ISBN-13: 9781234567890
ISBN-10: 1477123456

Cover design by: Art Painter
Library of Congress Control Number: 2018675309
Printed in the United States of America

Table of Contents

Preface

After writing my previous book, *Operational Risk Management - A Case Study Approach to Effective Planning and Response*, the experience was rewarding, but the time and energy devoted to its preparation were overwhelming. So, like many others who have gone down that road, I considered my book-writing days to be in the rearview mirror.

Little by little, however, book fatigue gave way to the realization that my area of interest - risk and resilience - required additional commentary as the world has become much more integrated and complex. Moreover, the new normal in which much of society thinks and behaves today, both as individuals and organizations, leaves a gap that needs to be filled by sound, practical guidance on how to navigate through the minefields of life.

The World According to Humpty Dumpty is intended to help fill that gap. The observations, lessons learned and takeaway messages are presented in a narrative that any audience can appreciate and apply to make more risk-informed decisions. It is my hope that your seat on your wall becomes less vulnerable and more resilient from the information contained herein.

There are many people to thank for their love, support and encouragement during what turned out to be a lengthy process to complete this effort. First and foremost are my family, my Mom, Susan, our children, their spouses, and grandchildren who, at various times, served as a source of inspiration, a welcome relief from writer's block, and editorial guidance (thanks Alyssa). I am also grateful for my colleagues at Vanderbilt - faculty, staff and students alike - for listening to my ideas and challenging them. That appreciation extends to my other professional relationships as well as my circle of friends, with a special shoutout to the CBers. And, finally, to my loved ones who are no longer with us, you set an example of life values I strive to live by.

Introduction

It is a simple nursery rhyme, of unknown origin, with the English version dating back to the late 1800s:

Humpty Dumpty sat on a wall
Humpty Dumpty had a great fall
All the King's horses and all the King's men
Couldn't put Humpty together again!

Many of us recited these lyrics as children and giggled our way through the thought of an animated egg falling off a wall and nobody could salvage the poor guy.

Fast forward to today and Humpty Dumpty is a profound representation of what we are currently experiencing. Our world is a complicated and volatile place. It is colored by pandemics, natural disasters, human atrocities, economic distress, geographic and political crises, and a variety of other challenges. Our education system is broken, financial institutions flip flop between being poorly managed and reaping large profits while manipulating the system on both ends, and home ownership is out of reach for many and too costly to keep for others. Single-parent households are no longer the exception, and we continue to guzzle gas and other fossil fuels to support our energy needs. We fret about the physical and emotional health of ourselves and our loved ones, worry that our freedoms are being compromised, fear for our public safety, lose sleep over whether we can pay the bills, and stress over the quality of our environment.

The truth is that each one of us is a Humpty Dumpty, living a fragile existence fraught with threats and vulnerabilities of all kinds. While we may be perched on different walls with varying levels of peril, we all face situations that could upend us, with the possibility of falling off our wall and not being able to recover. Not only to survive, but to thrive, we must adopt an approach that keeps us from falling while simultaneously being able to enjoy the view.

The truth is that each of us is a Humpty Dumpty, living a fragile existence fraught with threats and vulnerabilities of all kinds.

As much as it may seem that we live in the most trying of times, in reality we are just experiencing life, albeit with more twists and turns than our predecessors likely confronted. While the circumstances can rightfully be called a *new normal*, the truth is that risk has always been an inherent part of life. Humans have been taking risks in exchange for rewards ever since we inhabited the planet. The difference is that the risks we now face bombard us from many directions and at a frenetic pace, much of it attributable to a global economy and the rapid development of information technology. Like it or not, we are consumed with events in seemingly remote parts of the world that directly impact on our livelihood. Disaster awareness reaches our doorstep in real-time and in vivid detail, anyone's opinions or actions can go viral on the internet without notice, and we are constantly solicited by predators using scare tactics to exploit our time and money.

Years ago, a colleague told me that the key to dealing with this is to maintain a comfortable *pace*, the rate at which we digest information and act on it. Pace is something that we can often control; however, once relinquished, it is extremely difficult to regain. Maintaining a healthy pace is fundamental to managing our risks nowadays.

Imagine having your own *risk wheel*, rolling at a pace of your desired speed and direction. Envision this wheel as being comprised of a hub and spokes. The hub is your *risk control center*, a combination of how attuned you are to risk as a fundamental part of life, how cognizant you are to events that shape your risk perceptions, your corresponding appetite for accepting certain types of risks, and the decisions you make in responding to a risk that you deem to be unacceptable. Each spoke represents a different type of threat, which comes with the challenge of keeping that spoke intact in order for the wheel to continue to roll as intended. If any spoke weakens, your risk wheel will wobble and it will be difficult to maintain the desired pace. If the spoke breaks, the wheel falters, leaving you prone to potentially serious consequences.

> **Imagine having your own risk wheel, rolling at a pace of your desired speed and direction.**

How do you keep your risk wheel intact? Much of it depends on your level of control and how you are impacted by outside influences. To be successful, you must establish priorities and weigh decisions in terms of the risks and rewards relative to achieving them. This principle applies whether your circumstances are centered on family and friends, your work, the community where you live, or the broader landscape that defines your universe.

You have the power to be much more in the driver's seat in determining how your risk wheel rolls down the road of life than you perhaps realize. Your choices heavily influence whether you are able to maneuver through traffic without incident or find yourself spinning out of control.

The World According to Humpty Dumpty provides a clear and compelling perspective and offers simple, yet powerful, advice on how to successfully maintain control over the risks that you may encounter, even enabling you to leverage risk as an opportunity to embrace rather than dread over what might happen next. Some of what you read will help you understand how risks are perceived and acted upon, and what it takes to re-calibrate your focus on what truly matters. Special attention is devoted to emerging threats that are looming and which will require a proactive risk management approach to "nip them in the bud". The book concludes with easy-to-follow, actionable techniques for effectively managing your re-calibrated risk portfolio.

From the knowledge you gain, perhaps you can re-write this nursery rhyme as:

Humpty Dumpty sat on a wall
Humpty Dumpty never teetered at all
All the King's horses and all the King's men
praised Humpty for his risk acumen!

Part I - The Basics

The proper way to understand risk and how risk-informed decisions are made is to appreciate the fundamental aspects of what motivates our beliefs and actions. In this section, we cover that ground by introducing three connected topics: 1) how risk perceptions are formed, 2) communicating risk, and 3) what you should worry about.

How we form our perceptions of risk is based on a variety of factors that typically involve personal experiences or those of others. Collectively, these factors create a powerful sense of what we believe to be true, impacting the information we seek, how that information is processed, and what actions we are willing to take when encountering a potential threat.

Equally important is how we communicate risks to one another, and whether we are on the giving or receiving end of this discourse. When done effectively, communication can be the difference between successfully resolving a high-risk situation or letting it intensify with potentially serious outcomes.

When our perception of risks and what factual data tell us are not well-aligned, it leads to decisions on how to prioritize our risk management attention that can be way off the mark. As a result, we end up worrying about the wrong things and wasting precious resources, while more important concerns are given short shrift or ignored altogether.

How Risk Perceptions Are Formed

We all encounter stress in our daily lives. Many are minor and easily overcome, while other, rarer, circumstances can lead to more devastating impacts. Much of our ability to successfully manage these stressors relies on being able to make rational risk-informed decisions. Adopting this behavior is aided considerably by understanding how risk perceptions are formed and how those perceptions affect our personal and professional well-being.

Our risk perception is strongly influenced by the context in which we observe and absorb situations we encounter. Listed below are several key factors, in no particular order of importance, that can drive this process.

Does it affect me?
It matters whether a particular risk scenario poses a direct threat to you. If believe you are not exposed to that risk, it is less likely to be of concern. For example, if you don't smoke, the likelihood of contracting lung cancer diminishes significantly. Hence, your perceived risk of becoming a lung cancer victim will be relatively low compared to someone who has been a chain smoker their entire adult life. Similarly, if you are not into skydiving, the risk is immaterial because you do not engage in that activity. The same can be said for certain occupations, for example, underground mining. The risk of an explosion or collapse may weigh heavy on the minds of miners and their families, but is less likely to register with others who do not feel a direct connection.

Is it voluntary or imposed?
If you are forced to engage in an activity rather than participate voluntarily, your perception of the associated risk is likely to differ. The reason is simple; when acting on your own volition, you are freely making a decision to participate, whereas an imposed condition requires you to be involved, with the

possibility that you are expected to conform to a standard to which you may not agree or consider threatening. Therefore, you are likely to perceive less risk associated with an action you elect to take than one in which you are obligated to join.

Consider the management of spent nuclear fuel generated by commercial nuclear reactors. Many nations are advocating that the preferred approach is to bury this radioactive waste underground in a geologic repository, supposedly out of harm's way, while the fuel decays over a prolonged period of time. Some national governments, determined to build permanent underground repositories for this purpose, have attempted to designate these sites without consent of the affected communities. This involuntary imposition has caused many residents to have a heightened fear for their health and safety. In some instances, this increased level of perceived risk has created enough negative public sentiment that such imposed siting decisions have since been placed on hold or taken off the table.

Had the process been structured to allow for voluntary consent by the community, the outcome may have been different. Under those circumstances, the community may have carefully considered its health and safety risks relative to the economic development opportunities that might lead to job growth as well as improved risk mitigation services (fire, police, education, etc.), potentially leading to a decision to express interest in being selected.

Can I control the outcome?

It is human nature to want to control our own destiny. There is something innate about trusting our judgement and capabilities more than anyone else. It follows that if we feel greater control over the outcome of a certain activity, our perceived risk will be lower than if put in a situation where we feel somewhat or completely helpless.

A classic example of this effect is when a group of friends plan a road trip and must decide who will be behind the wheel. Many of us would prefer to be the driver than a passenger because of a desire to be in control of the vehicle and a belief that we can do so more capably than others.

When we don't feel in control, the risk tends to loom larger in our mind. It is precisely that feeling which causes some of us to be uneasy about flying to a destination rather than driving ourselves, because the pilot is controlling the vehicle in the one instance and we are in control in the other. Ironically, statistics indicate that traveling on a commercial aircraft is far safer than making the same trip by car.

Is it natural or manmade?

When something goes wrong that is human-caused, a common reaction is to look for someone to blame. It presents an opportunity to point a finger at the individual or organization we believe could have acted differently to either prevent the incident from occurring or limit the ensuing loss and damage. If we sense that a threat may materialize due to the irresponsible behavior of an individual or organization, our risk perception is heightened.

Natural disasters, however, are often viewed differently. The occurrence of an earthquake, for example, represents an event that is likely to be viewed as an act of God, and there is no convenient party to blame. As a result, we tend to be more accepting that such events are unavoidable, and therefore our perception of natural disaster risks reverts to how well humans react to the situation, and not whether the originating event could have been prevented by human intervention. Note that some of what drives natural disaster risk perception may be changing as evidence grows of a direct connection between human behavior and the propensity of extreme weather events.

Consider the following contrast. When the Great Sendai Earthquake in the Pacific Ocean generated a tsunami which devastated the coast of northern Japan in 2011, nobody questioned whether earthquakes can occur in that region capable of producing dangerous tsunamis. This might explain why many people are willing to live in earthquake-prone areas. By contrast, when the Chernobyl nuclear reactor accident occurred in Russia in 1986, blame for incident occurrence and the ensuing consequences was placed directly on the reactor designers, control operators and emergency responders. This single event had a profound impact on the perception of nuclear energy risk throughout the globe.

Are the impacts immediate or long-term?

A by-product of our fast-paced society is a desire to get things done quickly. This breeds a culture where our lens is fixated on short-term considerations, situations we believe to be important and urgent. What we sacrifice in adopting this approach is that any serious issue that is slow-growing, but can lead to dire effects in the future, is largely ignored. The fallout from this outlook is that we tend to perceive short-term risk as being more egregious and downplay our perception of longer-term risks.

However, these so-called important, but not urgent, issues can end up becoming far more problematic for future generations, and become evident at a time when there are fewer options available to mitigate those risks. Warming global temperatures, sea level rise and a greater frequency of heavy precipitation events are indicative of emerging long-term trends. Although there is a growing consensus that the impacts of these changes could be devastating and that we must do more now, a lack of political will, perhaps a by-product of a lower perceived risk, has curbed motivation to take necessary action. Hence, the perceived risk associated with climate change is diminished while the risk associated with a problem that is "here and now" is perceived to be greater by comparison.

How bad can it be?

The potential consequences of an undesirable event can weigh heavily on our risk perception. If the likely, or even worst case, scenario is believed to cause little or no harm, we perceive the risk to be of less concern. Conversely, if the outcome has the potential to be serious, or perhaps even catastrophic, regardless of whether the likelihood of occurrence is remote, the perceived risk can far exceed what a technical risk analysis might conclude.

What is fascinating about this risk perception factor is how easy it is for different people to view the same situation through a substantially different lens. Consider a child playing on a playground whose parent believes that the worst that can happen is that their child might skin a knee. Another parent with a child playing on the same playground could view the situation quite differently, one where their child could hit their head on a sharp object and end up seriously injured. Hence, a different perceived risk can arise even though both children are engaged in the same activity at the same location.

The conundrum that is most perplexing is a case where there is potential for a catastrophic outcome, even if the chance of occurrence is extremely rare, yet not impossible. Our risk perception can be molded into thinking that any event of that magnitude is certain to occur, despite the fact that such an outcome is highly improbable. For example, consider a decision of whether to get vaccinated to gain lifetime protection from contracting a destructive virus, knowing there is a chance that a particular side effect, deemed life-threatening, has been observed in far less than 1% of vaccinated people. Some people will decide that because there is the, albeit extremely small, chance they will die, the perceived risk becomes sufficiently alarming that they will opt not to get vaccinated, even though the consequences could result in a fatal outcome far more likely by comparison.

How certain is it to happen?
As the likelihood of experiencing an undesirable event grows, regardless of the potential outcome, our perceived risk also tends to rise. The mere notion that something bad is more likely to occur produces added stress and anxiety that fuels this process.

Suppose two coastal communities are located in the potential path of an oncoming hurricane. Meteorologists are forecasting that Community A has a 70% chance of being hit, while Community B has a 40% chance, and Community C has a 10% chance, all with the same hurricane strength. Given this information, residents of Community A would be expected to have a more heightened risk perception than those living in Community B, while people living in Community C have an even lower perceived risk.

Do I trust the information source?
Our confidence in the validity of information is another important risk perception factor. We are particularly susceptible nowadays to how various media outlets provide information. With such a vast number of available sources, media aggressively compete in real-time for our attention, often by sensationalizing stories or purposely communicating misinformation. The more that we see, read or hear about a disastrous event that has occurred, or learn of an impending threat with the potential for a catastrophic outcome, the more fearful we become, which alters our risk perception.

If an alien from another planet landed on Earth and tuned into today's media outlets for the first time, they would immediately become worried sick over the possibility of being murdered, going bankrupt, having a fatal traffic accident, or contracting a lethal disease, among other dangers.

Finding trustworthy sources of information creates an opportunity to form a risk perception that is more closely aligned with reality. Conversely, if the information sources are disingenuous or unscrupulous, it sows anxiety and fear that stokes a heightened risk perception.

> **Finding trustworthy sources of information creates an opportunity to form a risk perception that is more closely aligned with reality.**

How well do I understand the situation?

Fear of the unknown is a powerful force influencing risk perception. We tend to associate greater risk when confronted with situations that we have difficulty understanding. This is a particularly vexing problem given the rapid pace of economic, political, social and technological change that characterizes the world we live in.

Lack of knowledge creates a perception that there may be something hidden or complex that makes us vulnerable. Even with limited knowledge, one can become easily confused and wary. Our natural reaction in these instances is to perceive a heightened risk because there is no basis for believing that such concern is unnecessary.

One topic where this risk factor is prevalent involves the development of genetically modified crops. By modifying DNA using genetic engineering methods, scientists have been able to produce new agricultural crops purported to be more resistant to pests, diseases and drought. While we might think this discovery should be heralded as a major achievement, some of us may perceive eating genetically modified food as not safe. It is conceivable that this heightened risk perception is based on a lack of understanding of genetic engineering methods and safeguards that are in place.

There can be an exception to this rule, however, when someone is extremely knowledgeable about a situation and is well aware that there are serious dangers involved. Here, the individual can have a heightened risk perception based on their complete understanding of the activity. Workers in a meat packing plant might feel this way, given the amount of processing activity performed using dangerous equipment while standing on slippery floors.

How familiar am I with the risk?
If we have lived with a potentially risky situation for a while, our awareness and experience in that environment are likely to temper our perceived risk. By contrast, when placed in a situation we have not previously encountered, lack of familiarity can generate new fears and anxiety, transformed into a greater perceived risk.

Many of us, for example, are reluctant to walk alone in a neighborhood after dark for fear of being harmed or robbed. Yet residents of that neighborhood may be comfortable strolling on the same streets because of their familiarity with the area and knowing that it is safe.

Or consider our reaction, and therefore our risk perception, to acts of terrorism in the U.S. as opposed to other nations, such as Great Britain. Domestic terrorism in the U.S. is a relatively new phenomenon and our lack of familiarity with these acts has heightened our risk perception. By contrast, the Brits have been exposed to domestic terrorism for several decades, such that they may consider these acts as somewhat routine, and therefore more likely to accept them as part of the risks they incur on a regular basis.

Perceived risk can also be impacted by familiarity with someone who has fallen victim to an unfortunate event. Situations like this abound. If we know a cancer patient, for example, we are likely to associate a greater risk with this disease than otherwise. The same can be said if we know someone who lost their house in a flood, had their home burglarized or were involved in a serious automobile accident. The simple truth is that knowing someone who has experienced a traumatic event makes the prospect of such an event more real to us and turns up the volume on our risk perception meter.

Are the benefits worth the risk?

Another aspect that influences our perception of risk is whether we believe the "reward" to be sufficiently large to more than offset the amount of risk we would be incurring. In these instances, there is a tendency to perceive the risk as being lower than perhaps it is in reality. Conversely, if we feel there is little to gain or no benefit from incurring that same level of risk, it tends to heighten our perceived risk.

A heightened risk perception is often associated with the transportation of hazardous chemicals from a manufacturer to a customer. On the manufacturer end, producing the hazardous chemical generates employment and injects tax dollars into the local community. On the customer end, the chemicals are used by companies to make other products or for use in the service industry, again generating employment and a larger tax base. But what about the communities located along the transportation route used to carry the chemicals from the shipment origin to its destination? These people derive no benefit from the product moving through their jurisdiction, but incur the risk of a possible accident or intentional attack that leads to a product release with the potential to cause human casualties, business disruption and ecological destruction. The perceived risk of these shipments is likely to be much higher for residents and businesses in those transportation corridor communities than for populations located at either end of the shipment.

Being aware of the manner in which circumstances can shape our risk perception is important in how we assess the threats and outcomes associated with various risk scenarios. Additionally, it provides insight into opportunities to adjust our risk perception by acknowledging biases introduced by our sensitivity to these factors and working to re-calibrate towards achieving a more balanced perspective.

It is also important to recognize that the aforementioned factors can work in tandem in influencing our risk perception, while others may be at odds with one another. For example, if a risk is imposed on us and we don't know the potential severity of the outcome, the combined effect would likely serve to magnify our sense of heightened risk. By contrast, if a risk is imposed on us, but the impacts, if harmful, will not be experienced until years from now, these factors may serve to negate one another in shaping our perceived risk.

Besides ourselves, we must also consider how others we interact with form their risk perceptions. Knowing their risk perceptions and what shapes their attitudes and behaviors can mean the difference between creating conflict or finding common ground. This is a two-way street, though, as it applies to both how we communicate our views and how we interpret what others have to say.

A final thought. The larger the gap between perception and reality, the more likely it is that our risk mitigation resources will get misdirected. Under the adage that the "squeaky wheel gets the grease", the emotions associated with unjustifiably high perceived risks spawn a disproportionate amount of attention to be devoted to those matters, at the expense of applying the same resources that could be more effectively used to mitigate serious threats that are more grounded in realism.

> The larger the gap between perception and reality, the more likely it is that our risk mitigation resources are getting misdirected.

Communicating Risk

The context and manner in which risk is communicated impacts how it is absorbed by the recipient, and the extent to which it reinforces or alters their perceptions, attitudes and behaviors. The key to successful risk communication is recognizing there is no single audience, but rather a multitude of different audiences with whom you are conveying and receiving risk information. Moreover, some of these audiences are *internal*, people with whom you share an affiliation, while others are *external*, individuals with whom you may share a common interest.

From an organizational perspective, internal risk communication audiences may include staff, supervisors, senior managers and board members. External stakeholders can be rather diverse and might include business partners, regulators, elected officials, law enforcement and emergency responders, the public at large, and the media. Each audience is likely to have different agendas and objectives, yet may be critical to an organization's vitality and viability.

Personal audiences follow much the same pattern, but with different relationships. Your internal risk communication audience may consist of immediate and extended family members, close friends and advisors, and perhaps co-workers. External stakeholders might be neighbors, school teachers, religious leaders, doctors, social club members, elected officials, and local businesses.

Risk communication becomes challenging when realizing that each constituency comprises a population group who possess different communication needs. The public at large, for example, can be distinguished by age, ethnicity, income, gender, education, and other demographics. Each combination of these characteristics represents a potentially unique audience when devising an effective risk communication strategy. Would you explain risk the same way to a poor elderly man with little educational background whose primary language is not English, as you would to a young woman who is college-educated and owns a home in the suburbs? Navigating these circumstances is best served if we accept that each constituent group and sub-group is a "customer" who benefits from an individualized approach to communicating risk that ensures information is understood and well-received.

And if you don't accept this premise? The initial stage of this misunderstanding is likely to be confusion and conflict, as both parties are unable to see eye-to-eye. Confusion and conflict breed a desire for each party to defend its position, leading each side to exaggerate the truth by injecting personal biases into the conversation. With inaccurate information streaming from both sides, emotions escalate, creating an untenable situation. Eventually this can lead to gridlock, where nothing is accomplished and nobody benefits. But it is actually worse than that, for once gridlock sets in, the situation can become virtually impossible to unwind, with a best-case scenario being that a significant amount of time has to pass, years or even decades perhaps, before the issue can be re-introduced with some hope of resolution.

Below are some Rules of the Road to avoid traveling down this path when communicating risk:

Recognize each audience has varying levels of expertise, interest and attention span.

Put yourself in the shoes of the folks you are trying to reach with your risk information. How well do they know the subject matter? How much do they care about the risk? To what extent are they willing and able to listen to what you have to say? Responses to these questions will frame the type of audience you are addressing and how to customize the message. This applies to communicating risk as an organization or as an individual.

Make an effort to understand the needs of the people you are trying to reach.
Most successful marketing efforts are customer-driven and communicating risk is no different. Fundamental to this approach is treating your audiences as customers, and doing necessary background research to understand their needs and influences. Listen to their specific concerns, ask for input and ideas for resolution, and show respect for the feedback you receive. Importantly, realize that respecting someone's opinion shows that you value their input, but it does not mean that you have to agree with it.

Be honest, candid and open.
History has shown that when one tries to deceive an audience with misinformation, it is a losing proposition in the long run. Therefore, as painful as the truth may be when conveying risk information, it is important to be honest. It is equally important to be candid in the way information is presented and being open to reaction.

As much as you might sometimes think, your audiences are not as ignorant as they appear, and they are generally shrewd in their assessment of whether you and your message are trustworthy. And if you lose trust, all bets are off. Anything you say thereafter will be viewed through a lens of arrogance or malicious intent.

Consider the event involving a major spill from a diesel oil tank owned by the Ashland Oil Company. On January 2, 1988, the tank collapsed and failed, dumping an estimated one million gallons of diesel fuel into the Monongahela River several miles south of Pittsburgh, PA. The spill temporarily contaminated drinking water sources for people living in three states, infiltrated river ecosystems, killed wildlife, damaged private property, and adversely affected businesses in the area, in addition to spreading unpleasant odors.

John Hall, Ashland's chairman at the time, held an immediate press conference, against the advice of his corporate attorneys, in which he apologized for the spill, admitted his company made mistakes, showed concern and regret for the impact the spill was having on the community and environment, committed to paying for damages, and supported an outside investigation. By being honest, candid and open, Hall gained the confidence of government officials and the public, winning the admiration of crisis management experts for his character and demeanor. In doing so, he made a difficult situation more bearable rather than adding fuel to the fire.

Treat parties as legitimate partners in problem resolution. All too often, the parties with whom we are communicating risk information are considered opponents whose position needs to be marginalized in order to achieve a desired outcome. This is a wasted opportunity. Why? Because as an organization or as an individual, we do not own the market on good ideas. The organizations and people who are influenced by the risk in question have likely thought about how to alleviate the problem and may have devised their own ideas which are worthy of consideration. We would be doing everyone a disservice if those ideas are not allowed to reach the light of day. Moreover, by showing these audiences that you welcome their input, the process becomes more constructive and less likely to deteriorate into an "us versus them" scenario. Done correctly, risk communication can be a vehicle for producing more effective risk reduction strategies and actions.

Done correctly, risk communication can be a vehicle for producing more effective risk reduction strategies and actions.

Several years ago, I was involved in a situation where a state legislature approved a bill to designate transportation routes where certain high-hazard materials, such as explosives and poisonous-by-inhalation chemicals, would be allowed to travel. This had the potential to be contentious, as many stakeholders opposed the idea of incurring the risk of an accident while a high-hazard shipment passed through their community.

To their credit, the state agency assigned to make these routing decisions immediately formed a task force to help advise and guide the route evaluation and designation process. The task force was comprised of representatives from several audiences, including elected officials, businesses, citizen groups, chemical shippers, and freight transporters. The task force met at the outset of the initiative and frequently thereafter to review route assessment methods, findings and recommendations, and the state agency listened and incorporated task force feedback.

A preliminary set of designated routes was eventually produced, which were required to be presented at public hearings before being finalized. Several public hearings were scheduled, spread across the state so that access was proximate to anyone who cared to attend. Ordinarily, one would expect these hearings to attract a large attendance and discord. It did not happen. Instead, there was little to no participation at any of the public hearings, with the most significant concern raised by a county who disagreed with the recommended route to serve their jurisdiction. This situation was easily resolved because the assessment process had identified two other feasible routes in the county that were considered equally desirable. So, the state agency tasked the county to decide which of the three they would prefer, with an understanding that the county recommendation would be adopted.

In hindsight, the reason this potentially contentious risk scenario did not blow up can be traced to actions taken by the state agency at the outset and the manner in which it conducted business with the task force. By treating task force members as legitimate partners in problem identification and resolution, not only did the members feel a sense of ownership by being directly engaged in the process, but they also provided suggestions that led to a better result. Importantly, task force members served as liaisons to the audiences they represented, such that when the question was raised by their respective constituents whether to voice strong objections at the public hearings, they were able to communicate that the process was legitimate and that there was no need to question the result.

◆ ◆ ◆

One of the most deceiving ways in which risks are communicated is by publishing statistics that compromise the objectivity of the information. By committing this statistical communication bias, one promotes unfounded results to accentuate the importance of one position while hiding or compromising the truth. Depending on the source and motive, statistical communication bias can happen intentionally or quite by accident.

Depending on the source and motive, statistical communication bias can happen intentionally or quite by accident.

Two of the more common ways in which statistical communication bias emerges are through the reporting of the frequencies and rates of certain outcomes. Frequencies represent the number of events that occur in a given period of time and are typically used to compare different groups (e.g., number of fatalities due to cancer vs. heart disease) or changes in the same group over time (e.g., number of traffic deaths in present vs. previous calendar year). Rates are used to report changes in frequencies relative to a unit of output, such as population or number of miles traveled. Similar to frequency, rates can be used to interpret trends between or within specific populations over a specified period of time.

A popular form of statistical communication bias occurs when reporting changes in frequency, as illustrated below. In this hypothetical example, the number of people who have succumbed to two different diseases, Disease A and Disease B, are reported over similar time periods, X, Y and Z. Note that beginning in time period X, twice as many people died from Disease B (100) when compared to Disease A (50). When reporting the percentage change in fatalities for each disease by comparing time period X to time period Y, for both diseases there is a 100% increase in fatalities. If reported in this fashion alone, one would conclude that each disease grew by the same amount, hiding the fact that there was an increase of 100 fatalities associated with Disease B, while an increase of just 50 fatalities associated with Disease A. Based on the percent change alone, decision-makers might allocate the same amount of risk management resources to mitigate each disease, obscuring the fact that the Disease B likely deserves greater attention.

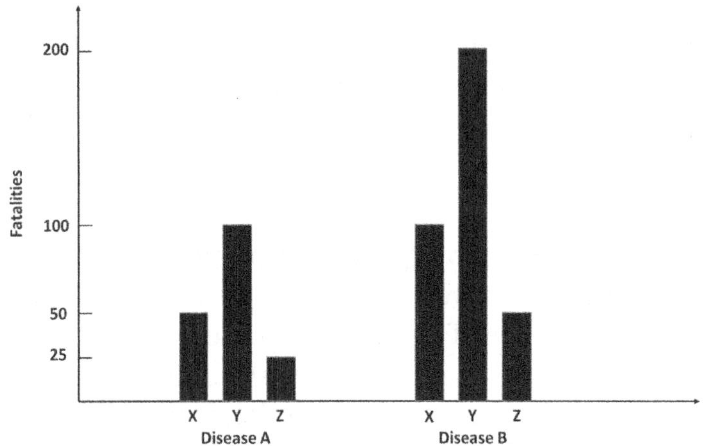

Changes in Disease Frequency

Statistical communication bias can act in the reverse as well. When reporting the percentage change in fatalities associated with each disease by comparing time period Y to time period Z, there is a 75% reduction in the number of fatalities for both diseases, yet there is a decrease of 75 fatalities for Disease A and 150 fatalities for Disease B.

A common statistical communication bias trap involving rates occurs when trying to individualize a risk that someone may encounter. Consider the hypothetical example below, where fatalities within a particular population are compared between calendar year 2010 and 2020. Looking at the fatality trend alone, one would conclude that between 2010 and 2020, fatalities have increased by 50%. However, observe that the population has also increased during that same time period. Using this information, the fatality rate per capita in 2010 is 0.20 while the fatality rate per capita in 2020 is 0.15. So, the likelihood that an individual in this population will die has actually decreased over the decade, even though the number of fatalities has increased during the same time. Statistical communication bias occurs here if the increase in fatalities is used solely as the reporting metric, misleading the audience into believing they are personally at greater risk now than before.

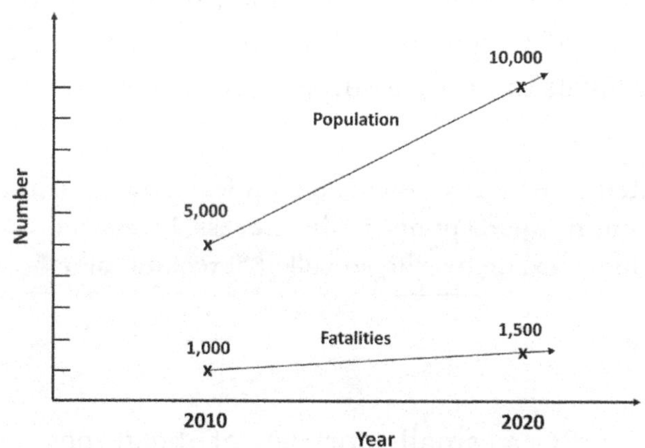

Population and Fatality Trends

The legendary Mark Twain once said, "Facts are stubborn things, but statistics are pliable." We must guard against the pliability of statistics so that statistical communication bias does not impair the quality of information we need to make effective risk-informed decisions.

◆ ◆ ◆

So much of our risk perception is fashioned around how we are informed by the media that this relationship warrants its own discussion. Simply put, the media is a powerful force in shaping opinion.

In its desire to gain market share, media engage in a cutthroat battle to out-hype the competition. Media do this by preying on our fears, manipulating our risk perceptions in the process, by constantly peppering us with so-called "breaking news" under the guise that something is always occurring in real-time that requires our undivided attention and immediate concern. The advancement of information technology has provided a global reach in the media quest for these sensational headlines, providing an ample supply of audio and video to help transmit the supposed gravity of a situation. And if by chance another breaking news story is not imminent, the potential consequences of rather normal occurrences are heightened to unrealistic levels to capture our attention.

> **Media do this by preying on our fears, manipulating our risk perceptions in the process, by constantly bombarding us with so-called "breaking news"...**

In reality, only a small portion of headlines correspond to a newsworthy item warranting such intense coverage. Unfortunately, the media has created such a heightened level of sensationalism to capture viewers and readers, it is unlikely to retreat to a more serene risk communication approach anytime soon.

While it is easy to blame the media for this phenomenon, the onus falls on us as well. We are the ones who have become conditioned to process information in sound bites, absorbing what we think we need to know in a matter of a few seconds to no more than a minute or two. This is hardly a time scale in which to evaluate the quality or context of what we are seeing or hearing. Complicating matters is that the human appetite for sensational news far outpaces our interest in hearing about potential disasters that were averted because of effective planning and decision-making.

To regain control of focusing on the risks that are truly of utmost concern, we must spend the time to challenge the information we are receiving by asking the right questions in formulating our views, including:

1. What is the source of the information being reported?
2. How accurate is the information?
3. How current is the information?
4. How likely could this information impact my life?

To answer these questions, we must dig deeper than simply reading headlines or brief blurbs about a purportedly high-risk situation. What we see or hear from a particular media source should be treated as a starting point in deciding whether it warrants a deeper dive into finding the facts. Use these snippets of media information as a screening process to hone in on how much it matters to you. The subset of those that you decide actually matter will help focus your time and energy on fact-finding, while eliminating the vast majority of what is being thrown at you and the confusion that comes with it.

From the perspective of an organization implementing a risk communication plan, media relations should be a fundamental and ongoing part of that effort. Maintaining continuity in communicating risk to the media during non-emergency times may be a difference maker when dealing with a future crisis. Continuity can be achieved by issuing regular press releases that provide background information the media can source in the event of an incident. Additionally, having risk managers available for media access on an ongoing basis during non-emergency times will lend credibility when an emergency occurs. Why? Because the media will gravitate towards people they already know for timely information during an emergency rather than turning to a less familiar source.

Most of us take the aspect of communicating risk too lightly, treating it merely as sharing our beliefs or opinions without regard to the nuances that can seriously impact how information is received and digested. This creates an environment where the risk in question is often poorly understood and can lead to wildly inaccurate perceptions and subsequent irrational behavior. And this is a two-way street, as we are potential victims of both failing to properly communicate risk as well as having risks communicated to us that fall short of what we truly need to know.

As discussed earlier, the key to effective risk communication is recognizing that no single audience exists, but rather a multitude of different audiences with whom we interact when communicating risk. To be successful, we must treat each audience as a customer who requires an individualized approach such that the information we convey is understood and well-received. This requires an appreciation and respect for their needs, and a willingness to communicate in an honest, candid and open manner. By doing so, you may be surprised at the progress one can make in mitigating the risk in question, with the possibility that the preferred approach may even come from an idea floated by a member of your audience rather than yourself.

The inability to adopt this approach can lead to a rapid ratcheting up of emotions, creating a downward spiral which can become so contentious that finding common ground becomes virtually impossible and long delays are incurred before the matter can even be brought forward again for resolution. This predicament is typically aided by the proliferation of inaccurate or distorted information as each side tries to embolden their position, further fueled by media that is anxious to sensationalize the situation.

As we wrap up with this discussion, I leave you with the following quote attributed to George Bernard Shaw, "The single biggest problem in communication is the illusion that it has taken place." For many of the risks we encounter today, we simply cannot afford to suffer from this malady.

What Should I Worry About?

It is always interesting to compare our perceptions of what we should worry about as a society with what credible statistical information tells us. You will likely be surprised by the difference in the results.

In a risk management course that I teach, early in the semester I present students with a list of various causes of death in the U.S. and ask them to rank order the lifetime odds of death associated with each cause. You can try this for yourself right here if you like.

- Bicyclist
- Chronic Lower Respiratory Disease
- Cancer
- Choking on Food
- Dog Attack
- Motor Vehicle Crash
- Hornet, Wasp and Bee Stings
- COVID-19
- Pedestrian Incident
- Electrocution, Radiation, Extreme Temperatures, and Pressure
- Suicide
- Drowning
- Fire or Smoke
- Sunstroke
- Heart Disease
- Motorcyclist
- Guns
- Fall
- Hot surfaces and substances
- Opioid Overdose
- Sharp Objects
- Cataclysmic Storm

Note that the risk metric being used is the lifetime odds of death. This measure is commonly used to report societal health risk. It is popular for several reasons: 1) death is the most undesirable outcome associated with injury and disease, 2) everyone has to die sometime, so the sum of the probabilities for all causes must equal one, and 3) government data collection agencies consistently track and report this information.

Now let's compare your rank ordering with the government data. The table below displays the lifetime odds of death in the U.S. for the aforementioned causes based on the most recent reporting by the National Safety Council .

It is important to recognize that lower numbers equate to higher odds. For example, based on 2021 data, the lifetime odds of dying from chronic lower respiratory disease is 1 in 31, while the odds of dying from a motor vehicle crash is 1 in 93, meaning that dying of chronic lower respiratory disease is three times more likely.

How well did you do? Are you surprised that some of the risks you considered as relatively high are actually much lower, or vice-versa?

From a risk management perspective, there are several important takeaways in reviewing this information. First, it provides an understanding of where risk management resources might be best allocated. For example, for every dollar spent, would it make more sense to mitigate the risk of suicide than bicycle incidents? While this doesn't mean that lower risk categories should be completely ignored, it can provide a persuasive argument for allocating a disproportionate amount of risk management resource toward more highly ranked causes.

Lifetime Odds of Death in the United States by Select Cause, 2021

Cause of Death	Odds of Dying
Heart disease	1 in 6
Cancer	1 in 7
COVID-19	1 in 10
Chronic lower respiratory disease	1 in 31
Opioid overdose (accidental)	1 in 58
Guns (all intents)	1 in 89
Suicide	1 in 91
Motor-vehicle crash	1 in 93
Fall	1 in 98
Pedestrian incident	1 in 485
Motorcyclist	1 in 747
Drowning	1 in 1,006
Fire or smoke	1 in 1,287
Choking on food	1 in 2,659
Bicyclist	1 in 3,546
Sunstroke	1 in 4,655
Electrocution, radiation, extreme temperatures, and pressure	1 in 13,176
Cataclysmic storm	1 in 20,098
Sharp objects	1 in 25,960
Hot surfaces and substances	1 in 45,908
Dog attack	1 in 53,843
Hornet, wasp, and bee stings	1 in 54,516

A second important observation comes not from reviewing this table alone, but rather comparing the results with another period of time, say five years earlier. When doing so, we can analyze trends over time, allowing us to highlight the direction in which a particular risk is heading - improving, deteriorating or staying more or less the same. If an improving trend is observed, it could be that previously implemented risk mitigation strategies are proving effective or that other risks are becoming more prominent. Conversely, a deteriorating trend suggests that more attention may need to be devoted to mitigating a growing risk before it becomes even more difficult to manage. A flat trend suggests that the situation has remained relatively static which, depending on its current risk level, can mean that the situation is under control and additional risk mitigation is not needed, or that the situation remains dire and previously implemented risk mitigation strategies, if any, have proven ineffective.

The previous discussion presents a broad overview by treating the U.S. population as one homogeneous group. In reality, we are each distinguishable by a variety of personal characteristics that alter these odds. Among the common characteristics influencing these odds are origin, race, age, sex and employment. Also, not everyone engages in the same activities (e.g., motorcycle riding), or at the same level (e.g., daily vs. once in a while). By differentiating according to these characteristics, the statistical information is more likely to align with the risks that we face.

To illustrate this point, consider the table below published by the National Center for Health Statistics, which displays U.S. fatality rates per 100,000 population in 2022, by race, Hispanic origin and sex. Note that these are age-adjusted fatality rates, meaning that the ages of people in each population group are factored into the computation, such that the overall rates are based on the same age structure.

2022 Age-Adjusted Death Rates by Race, Hispanic Origin and Sex: Rates per 100,000 Population

Hispanic	Male	Female
	774.2	512.9
Non-Hispanic		
AIAN*	1,444.1	1,063.6
Asian	522.2	354.9
Black	1,263.3	813.2
White	971.9	691.9

* American Indian or Alaska Native

This table indicates that the highest death rates in 2022 were associated with the American Indian or Alaska Native population. For the non-Hispanic population, individuals classified as being part of the Asian population had the lowest death rate, followed by White and Black populations, respectively. There is also a notable distinction when reviewing fatality rates by sex, with females having a much lower rate, irrespective of race or Hispanic origin.

Risks associated with various types of employment can be reflective of the occupational hazards associated with working in different business types. The table below, produced by the U.S. Bureau of Labor Statistics, captures this relationship in terms of the 2021 fatality rate for select industry sectors.

2021 Fatality Rate by Select Industry Sector

Industry	Fatality Rate per 100,000 Workers	Number of Fatalities
Agriculture, forestry, fishing, and hunting	19.5	453
Mining	14.2	95
Transportation and warehousing	14.2	976
Construction	9.4	986
Wholesale trade	5.1	177
Professional and business services	1.4	242
Retail trade	1.9	263
Information	1.5	36
Other services	3.8	383
Manufacturing	2.6	383
Leisure and hospitality	2.4	243
Government	2.4	461
Utilities	3.4	36
Financial activities	0.9	97
Education and health services	0.7	167

According to this data, agriculture, forestry, fishing and hunting; mining; transportation and warehousing; and construction emerge as much riskier professions than the other industries listed in the table. This makes sense given that people employed in those sectors are doing considerable manual labor, working with heavy equipment, exposed to natural hazards, and performing arduous tasks.

As we learned in the previous chapter, while rates are important for measuring the respective risk of individuals or organizations who are associated with a specific statistical group, rates alone should not be the basis for determining how to allocate risk management resources. Frequencies are also important, because while rates may indicate the risk for any specific individual associated with a statistical group, if the population of the statistical group is large enough, there may be more undesirable outcomes involving that group even if the rate is relatively low. A prudent approach would be to factor both rate and frequency into the risk management calculus in coming to terms with how to establish policy and investment priorities.

To emphasize this point, note that in the previous table the 2021 fatality rate for workers in the Agriculture, Forestry, Fishing and Hunting profession was 19.5 per 100,000 workers, while the rate in the Construction industry was 9.4 per 100,000 workers. On this basis alone, one would think that roughly twice as much risk management attention should be devoted to improving safety among Agriculture, Forestry, Fishing and Hunting workers. Yet in this same year, the Construction industry experienced more than twice as many fatalities as lives were lost among Agriculture, Forestry, Fishing and Hunting workers.

The primary intent of this chapter has been to demonstrate the gap that can exist between our perception of the significance of various risks and what credible data tells us. As our ultimate goal should be for perceived risk and credible statistical risk to be closely aligned, risks that present a sizeable gap between our perception and factual data are serious candidates for imparting risk education and awareness.

...our ultimate goal should be for perceived risk and credible statistical risk to be closely aligned...

It is also apparent that we need to customize our approach to risk assessment in a way that reflects personal characteristics and circumstances, taking both rates and frequencies into account. Our demographics, activities and activity levels all play a role in increasing or decreasing our exposure and vulnerability, and consequently the risks we incur. This requires the pursuit of quality and in-depth information necessary to support effective risk-informed decision-making.

As useful as this discussion may be, it reflects recent past history and is not necessarily indicative of what to expect in the future. Our risk world is undergoing a rapid transformation, with several new threats emerging that could have serious ramifications. These elephants in the room are our next topics of conversation.

Part II - Looming & Growing

How much we worry about what is right in front of us can obscure growing threats with potentially serious consequences if they are put off until a later time. Even if we are aware, the problem may seem too difficult to tackle, making it convenient to pretend it does not exist, in effect "kicking it down the road" for others to deal with in the future. These so-called *elephants in the room* have become plentiful in today's world. In this section, we focus on several of the more high-profile elephants: 1) climate change and extreme weather, 2) cybersecurity, 3) social networking, 4) infectious diseases, 5) domestic terrorism, and 6) geopolitical conflict.

Beyond their individual and collective impact on our risk portfolio, an unfortunate by-product of the stress and anxiety associated with these elephants is the insidious effect they can have on our mental health. Arguably, it is this cascading effect that presents the most problematic risk of all.

Adapting to Climate Change and Extreme Weather

We begin this discussion with an explanation of the relationship between climate and weather. The National Oceanic and Atmospheric Administration (NOAA) considers weather to be short-term changes in the atmosphere, whereas climate describes what the weather is like over a long period of time in a specific location. Climate change essentially drives changes in the weather patterns we experience. For the sake of convenience, we will use the term *climate risk* to denote the risks associated with both climate change and the extreme weather it generates.

A clear trend has emerged over the past several decades showing that Earth's climate is changing. The evidence is compelling. According to the Intergovernmental Panel on Climate Change (IPCC), the planet is experiencing warming temperatures, sea level rise, and retreating snow and ice cover, among other impacts. This, in turn, has caused significant changes in the frequency and severity of extreme weather, including heat waves, heavy precipitation events, droughts, and hurricanes, as well as severe storms that spawn tornados, hail, lightning and high winds. Moreover, future predictions suggest this trend will continue unabated and perhaps accelerate. Already there is no location on the planet immune to climate risk.

Many of these events produce catastrophic impacts in terms of human casualties, property damage and environmental destruction. Just in 2022 alone, NOAA recorded 18 separate weather and climate disasters costing at least 1 billion dollars of loss and damage. Such a large amount of loss and damage, as catastrophic as it appears, doesn't even consider the indirect and intangible effects that can cripple an entire region; more on that later.

Climate risk is viewed by many as the most existential threat facing the human race. If we don't address it now, experts argue, and with vigor, it will be a losing battle. This uphill climb is further complicated by the lack of political will to forge a full-frontal attack on the crisis. The glimmer of hope is that we have the ability to motivate a stronger desire for political movement by addressing the issue in a manner where everyone can see benefit in taking constructive action. Here's how.

Climate risk is viewed by many as the most existential threat facing the human race.

As it relates to climate risk, there are three types of believers: 1) our climate is not changing and what we are currently experiencing in terms of the frequency and severity of climate-related events is similar to what we have witnessed in the past (i.e., climate denier), 2) our climate is changing, but the human race is not responsible for causing this change (i.e., something we can't control), or 3) our climate is changing and we are responsible, in full or in part, for causing this change (i.e., we have some control over our destiny).

Let's take the first type of believer. Suppose that our climate is in a steady state, meaning that we don't anticipate that future conditions will undergo any meaningful change relative to the recent past. With the ongoing influx of population and new development in locations already considered at high risk, in addition to the growing replacement costs associated with damage or destruction to existing structures, the same events that have occurred in the past will render greater loss and damage in the future.

Now suppose one believes that our climate is changing, but the human race is not responsible for causing this change.

These individuals acknowledge that due to a changing climate, we can expect more frequent and severe climate-related events. This translates into the aforementioned population and infrastructure located in high-risk areas incurring greater loss and damage more often than in the past. Moreover, new areas will become designated as high risk due to the frequency and intensity of future events covering a larger land mass.

Finally, we come to the group of believers who acknowledge a changing climate and blame mankind for creating this problem. The only distinction between this group and the previous one is that there is a desire to act aggressively to decarbonize our environment by relying less on fossil fuels and using cleaner energy, lowering energy demand, and applying techniques for absorbing and storing carbon. Despite these efforts, however, this group of believers also acknowledge that before we can repair a deteriorating climate, for the next few decades the trend of increasing event frequency and intensity will continue.

The undeniable conclusion is that your climate politics shouldn't matter when it comes to the need to invest in strategies to reduce climate risk. While each group of believers may disagree as to the urgency and level or type of investment, pursuing the "low hanging fruit" is in everyone's best interest.

...your climate politics shouldn't matter when it comes to the need to invest in strategies to reduce climate risk.

The benefits of pursuing low hanging fruit cannot be overstated, for we don't really know the full extent of the consequences of climate-induced events. As discussed earlier, most of the loss and damage data recorded today focuses almost exclusively on human casualties and property damage, and omits consideration of indirect and intangible impacts. Examples of indirect impacts include loss of industrial production, traffic and supply chain disruption, and emergency costs. Intangible consequences include impacts such as long-term health effects, environmental destruction, inconvenience of post-event recovery, economic decline and loss of social connectedness. These indirect and intangible impacts when combined with human casualties and property damage, make an even more compelling case for an urgent need to manage climate risk.

By taking a more proactive stance, there can be added benefit beyond the prospect of accruing savings due to avoided disaster costs. Indications are that investing in climate risk reduction can also serve as a stimulus by providing opportunities to spur job growth and other forms of economic development.

In the sections to follow, we address in greater detail how to manage the risks associated with several climate-induced threats that are experienced in many areas of the world.

Flood

Floods are the most common and costly climate-induced disasters worldwide. Although these events are typically characterized by heavy precipitation, there are different types of floods and corresponding contributing factors. They can be episodic or occur over a longer duration, affecting a highly localized area or spanning a larger region.

Floods are the most common and costly climate-induced disasters worldwide.

Flash flooding is one type of episodic event, caused by an excessive amount of precipitation falling in a short period of time. Ground and stormwater management systems are unable to absorb and handle such short, intense storms. These events create significant runoff that can rapidly accumulate in low-lying areas. Conditions favorable for flash flooding include if the ground is already saturated when the precipitation event occurs and is therefore unable to absorb additional water, or following periods of drought where the soil denies water penetration due to excessive dryness.

Riverine flooding is an inland phenomenon that occurs when water levels rise over the top of river banks due to excessive rain from a specific precipitation event, persistent storms in the same area over an extended period of time, or combined runoff from rainfall and snowmelt. Riverine flooding can also occur in communities located downstream from where a flooding event initially begins. Additionally, failure of flood management infrastructure, such as dams and levees, can create flood scenarios due to excessive water volume and pressure.

Coastal inundation is a different beast, one that can wreak havoc due to a variety of factors. Often this begins with exposure to hurricanes and tropical storms that bring heavy precipitation and storm surge. When combined with sea level rise, land subsidence and diminishing natural ocean barriers, it creates a hostile environment for water levels to infringe on low-lying areas. While virtually all coastlines are at greater risk of flooding, some even flood regularly now due to high tides associated with a rising sea level. Certain locations are particularly perilous, in particular the U.S. Gulf Coast.

Flooding can ravage a community in many ways. Victims can drown in raging floodwaters. Buildings can incur structural damage due to the depth and force of flood waters, while electrical and heating, ventilation and air conditioning (HVAC) systems can be compromised after becoming wet. Mold and mildew can also damage building materials and its contents, creating an additional human health hazard. Flooded roadways and bridges can prevent emergency responders from accessing affected areas, block individuals from reaching safety, and restrict personal mobility. These risks are particularly acute for socially vulnerable populations (e.g., elderly, young, impoverished, lack of car ownership, etc.). Additionally, floodwaters can carry debris such as logs and other large objects, hazardous materials and sewage, carcasses of dead animals or people, and poisonous snakes.

Secondary and regional flood impacts include severed supply chains when segments of the transportation system become impassable. Indirect impacts of flooding can also include loss of wages from missed work days, physical illness, and stress-related mental health issues.

Agricultural areas are particularly prone to flood risk. Many field crops are planted in low-lying areas due to the fertility of the soils and access to water for irrigation. These lands can flood at prime times in the crop growing season, affecting yield and sometimes completely destroying crops. This can leave farmers with significant financial burden, and possibly bankruptcy, without an adequate income source. In addition, livestock can succumb to swift flood waters, by being cut off from food supplies, or lacking veterinary care for an extended period of time. Transportation system impacts due to flooding can also limit a farmer's ability to ship products to market.

Flood risk management has traditionally focused on designing culverts and stormwater infrastructure based on historic precipitation data, tied to the concept of a 100-year precipitation event. A 100-year event refers to rainfall totals that have a 1% chance of occurring at a specific location in any particular year. The use of a 100-year event in flood risk management utilizes the premise that if a location is designed to withstand a precipitation event of such magnitude, one where the odds if it happening are that small, then we have a built-in margin of safety corresponding to such an unlikely event.

But what if we are experiencing more frequent and heavier precipitation events, and this trend is expected to continue in the future? If this holds true, tomorrow's 100-year event will be larger in magnitude and geographical scale, potentially overwhelming areas already in flood zones, as well as locations we have been led to believe are not threatened. The loss and damage incurred in these supposedly impervious areas will be exacerbated by the continued development that has been taking place because of the false notion that the area is safe.

If the 100-year event continues to be our risk management standard, it is incumbent on flood managers to re-calibrate the amount of precipitation that will be associated with a future 100-year event. They should then take the necessary steps to not only protect the vulnerability of communities and infrastructure located in this more expanded area, but to discourage new development as well.

Flood risk management strategies can range in terms of the size of the investment and whether it is implemented at the individual, organizational or community level. Below is a list of strategies worthy of consideration:

- Increase greenspace and pervious areas to absorb and slow runoff from heavy precipitation events. This can be accomplished by encouraging homeowners and businesses to use pervious pavers or gravel for driveways and parking lots as opposed to pavement or asphalt. Additionally, creating natural buffers around streams and rivers can help slow flood waters and increase absorption.
- Implement low impact development policies. Such policies require developers to reduce the potential for runoff to flood stormwater or sewer systems by capturing it on-site for gradual release or re-use, using detention basins/ponds or other green infrastructure.
- Prevent development in floodplains and remove people/

structures that are in high flood risk areas. Regulations that prohibit or restrict development in floodways (as defined by flood insurance rate maps or otherwise) can reduce the number of people and infrastructure assets at risk.

- Protect critical infrastructure located in or near floodplains. Water and wastewater treatment plants, natural gas pipelines, roads, bridges, etc. are often situated in close proximity to flood-prone areas. Hardening or protecting these assets with levees, floodwalls, or ensuring that redundancies (back-up systems) are in place will allow for flooding to occur with less impact. Power systems for pumps and other equipment used for water and wastewater treatment systems should be elevated above anticipated flood levels.
- Enhance public education and awareness. Most flood-related deaths are attributed to people not heeding warnings or trying to cross flood waters unsuccessfully in vehicles. Individuals need to be educated on flash flooding and how to stay safe when such situations arise. They also need to be aware of community resources, such as shelters.
- Invest in a multi-faceted approach to warning citizens, including methods to reach socially vulnerable populations.
- Create system redundancies. Distribute emergency response personnel and equipment throughout the region so that individuals needing help are not cut off due to flooding. This includes ensuring that alternative routes are available for both residents and emergency response personnel.
- Institute a freeboard requirement (the additional amount of height above the base flood elevation) that mandates the finished floor elevation in a structure to be higher than anticipated flood levels.

While some communities are initiating various types of flood risk management activities, it is not occurring at the rate or scale that are needed. Aiding and abetting this situation are several factors: 1) government policies that encourage development in high-risk flood areas while losses are subsidized nationally, 2) difficulty in taking private property for public use even when compensation is involved, 3) inability to communicate the urgency associated with climate risk, and 4) lack of incentives or mandates for federal, state and local managers to work together.

Drought

Drought, or an absence of water, is more formally defined as a period of below average precipitation in a given location, resulting in prolonged shortages in water supply, whether it be from precipitation, surface water or ground water. A drought can last for months or years, although it may be declared after only a several week period.

Lack of precipitation is a key factor in contributing to drought conditions. This creates an environment where the rate of water usage exceeds nature's ability to replenish the water supply. Water usage is associated with the allocation of surface water (rivers, streams, reservoirs, lakes) to support irrigation, navigation, power generation, recreation, habitat, and municipal drinking consumption. Areas reliant on groundwater can suffer from drought similarly to surface water supply locations. However, areas utilizing surface waters can often see a replenishment of the supply more directly through precipitation, whereas groundwater supplies require aquifer recharge that can take years or decades.

Drought impacts are felt across many populations and industry sectors. Extended drought can lead to human casualties, both directly or indirectly, due to dehydration, malnutrition and associated diseases. In rural areas heavily dependent on agriculture production, drought can prove devastating to crop productivity and survival, especially in warm summer months when crops typically grow more rapidly. Livestock may also become emaciated or die due to lack of water or diminished food sources. Impacts to infrastructure systems include both reduced flows for hydropower or cooling water for other power generation activities. Low flows in navigable waterbodies can limit or halt cargo movements, which in turn can cause supply chain disruptions for those depending on timely deliveries. Additional impacts may include water shortage for industrial use, damage to habitat (both terrestrial and aquatic), reduced water quality due to lower flushing of aquatic systems, and even brownouts or blackouts due to strains on energy production.

Developing risk management strategies is challenging in that drought typically is not a localized event, and it is difficult to accurately predict when it will start or end. Central to managing the impact of drought is to ensure access to adequate water supplies for essential services, which may be accomplished by taking the following actions:

- Install high quality backup wells to help meet critical drinking water needs in areas where surface water is primarily used for water supply.
- Enlist partner agencies who can provide bottled water or potable water in tanks.
- Provide water conservation public education and outreach prior to a drought to help prepare citizens and businesses on how to best utilize limited available water supplies.
- Employ rainwater harvesting and storage from rooftops to help provide water supply.
- Where possible, collect gray water (water from showers and handwashing) and repurpose for irrigation. Using recycled wastewater that has been properly treated can

also provide water supply for purposes such as crop irrigation and in some cases, with suitable treatment, utilized for potable water.

- Diversify crops, plan crop rotation to minimize erosion, and invest in drought-resistant species to reduce agricultural impacts. This can be accomplished in part through support provided by local agricultural extension agencies to help identify alternative crops that are both drought resistant and economically attractive for area farmers.

◆ ◆ ◆

Extreme Heat

Extreme heat injures or kills more people in the U.S. than any other climate-related event. It is extremely important to understand that temperature alone is not a sufficient measure of the impact of heat on the human body. A number of other factors weigh in, including whether a person is situated in direct sun or shade, type of clothing worn, relative humidity, and level of physical exertion.

Extreme heat injures or kills more people in the U.S. than any other climate-related event.

The heat index was developed to address some of these factors. It represents a measure of what the temperature feels like to the human body when relative humidity is combined with the air temperature. As shown in the chart below published by the U.S. National Weather Service, high air temperature, when combined with high humidity, can be devastating to the human body when the air temperature alone may be bearable. For example, if the air temperature is 96°F with 65% humidity, the heat index, what it feels like to our body, is 121°F.

Temperature (°F)

Relative Humidity (%)	80	82	84	86	88	90	92	94	96	98	100	102	104	106	108	110
40	80	81	83	85	88	91	94	97	101	105	109	114	119	124	130	136
45	80	82	84	87	89	93	96	100	104	109	114	119	124	130	137	
50	81	83	85	88	91	95	99	103	108	113	118	124	131	137		
55	81	84	86	89	93	97	101	106	112	117	124	130	137			
60	82	84	88	91	95	100	105	110	116	123	129	137				
65	82	85	89	93	98	103	108	114	121	128	136					
70	83	86	90	95	100	105	112	119	126	134						
75	84	88	92	97	103	109	116	124	132							
80	84	89	94	100	106	113	121	129								
85	85	90	96	102	110	117	126	135								
90	86	91	98	105	113	122	131									
95	86	93	100	108	117	127										
100	87	95	103	112	121	132										

Likelihood of Heat Disorders with Prolonged Exposure and/or Strenuous Activity

Caution ■ Extreme Caution ■ Danger ■ Extreme Danger

Heat Index Chart

Note that any day in which the heat index ranges between 103°F and 124°F is dangerous, with heat cramps or heat exhaustion likely, and heat stroke possible with prolonged exposure and/or physical activity. A heat index at or above 125°F is extremely dangerous with heat stroke becoming highly likely. Importantly, like traditional air temperature measurement, heat index values are premised on air temperature in the shade and assume light wind, such that exposure to full sunshine would have higher heat index values by up to 15°F.

The U.S. Centers for Disease Control and Prevention (CDC) defines four degrees of illness, varying according to heat severity: 1) rash, 2) cramps, 3) exhaustion, and 4) stroke. Whereas heat rash and cramps may be an indication of a more serious condition, they are generally treatable without seeking immediate medical attention. Heat exhaustion is a condition that tends to manifest itself over time when someone has been exposed to consistently high temperature, often without sufficient replacement of fluids.

While the aforementioned conditions can be serious, the greatest human health threat comes from heat stroke. It occurs when our body is no longer able to control its temperature through the normal sweating process. Unable to cool down, body temperature can damage the brain or other vital organs in as short a period of time as 10 to 15 minutes. This can lead to death or permanent disability.

The U.S. National Weather Service defines a heat wave as a period of abnormally hot weather generally lasting more than two days. Heat waves can pose serious risks to human health, particularly to children under four years of age, people age 65 or older, those who are overweight, and individuals who have other illnesses or are taking certain medications.

Extreme heat risk is expected to grow dramatically in the coming years. Climate change experts have been warning for some time about the onslaught of global warming and more frequent air temperature extremes. For example, in west Tennessee, historical records indicate that from 1950 to 1980, this region experienced an average of 14 days per year above 95°F and 2 days above 100°F. Based on current trends, by the middle of this century, the World Climate Research Programme projects that there will be 56 days on average every year of above 95°F and 14 days of above 100°F.

Increases in extreme heat can be expected to have profound impacts on hospital admissions and outdoor worker productivity. Extreme heat can also compromise infrastructure integrity, increase air pollution levels, damage crops, and promote bacterial or algae growth in water bodies, potentially impacting marine ecosystems.

A variety of strategies have been proposed in an attempt to control this risk:

- Invest in technology and coordinate closely with weather service agencies to provide more advanced detection, warning and communication of extreme heat events.
- Conduct public outreach and education to individuals most vulnerable to extreme heat, such as the elderly or

outdoor workers.

- Prioritize the allocation of extreme heat mitigation resources to locations with higher per-capita heat stress hospital visit rates.
- Create an inventory of critical infrastructure that may be vulnerable to significant increases in extreme heat; follow up with detailed inspections to determine if there are cost-effective risk reduction strategies that could be employed.
- Provide air-conditioned shelters and access to water for those in need (local businesses could partner with local governments to help in this regard).
- Start heat education early, so children understand the impacts of heat on their bodies, and can begin to advocate for themselves or advise others, such as their parents, on heat stress preparedness.

Wildfire

How a wildfire starts and the harm it renders involves a complex relationship among climate and weather factors, forest management practices, natural ecosystems, and the human-built environment. The largest fires have historically occurred in the western part of the U.S., characterized by high fuel load, wind speed and ambient temperature, combined with low fuel moisture and humidity. With many of these factors exacerbated by rising temperatures and increases in the duration and intensity of drought, the future appears ominous.

Not only do wildfires destroy property and threaten human safety, but according to the U.S. Geological Survey, secondary effects can also be devastating. These include fire-induced erosion and landslides, the introduction of invasive species, and changes in water quality. Population growth and infrastructure development encroaching on areas known to pose high wildfire risk are to a large extent responsible for these outcomes.

It is important to recognize that wildfires are part of a natural process that allows forests to maintain their vitality. Wildfires serve to "clean house" by removing leaves, logs and needles from the forest floor. They also thin out the overhead forest canopy, providing increased sunlight that helps new plants to grow. It is this cycle that enables a forest to remain healthy over long periods of time. When this natural housecleaning is not allowed to occur, it leads to a buildup of vegetation, creating a larger amount of combustible fuel to stoke a more severe fire when it eventually occurs.

Various government entities have a role in mitigating and responding to wildfires. In the U.S., states are responsible for responding to wildfires that occur on local, state or private lands, while the federal government manages fires that begin on federal lands. This delineation can cause confusion as to who is in charge of the response effort, particularly as a fire spreads, and underscores the importance of communication and interoperability among these agencies.

A recent study performed in response to the well-known Camp Fire in California identified important factors within government control to mitigate wildfire risk, in particular the importance of integrating and updating building codes and fire hazard maps. The Camp Fire was the costliest disaster worldwide in 2018, causing 85 deaths and destroying more than 18,000 buildings. In 2008, the State of California passed a law mandating the installation of fire-resistant roofs for new construction located in high fire hazard zones, areas defined by maps created in the late 1990s, based on now outdated climate information. While the 2008 building code appears to have contributed to saving a significant percentage of homes, nearly one-half of the those built to the "better" 2008 standard were still destroyed.

As a result, California is developing new fire hazard zone maps using updated climate and weather information as well as more current development data. With California taking the lead in promoting more proactive wildfire risk management, other states will hopefully follow suit, in response to the preponderance of wildfires occurring elsewhere.

Among the strategies to improve wildfire risk management are the following:

*Integrate updated climate and weather data into fire building codes for homes and businesses located in high fire hazard areas.

*Engage and incentivize local governments to redraw fire hazard zones and adopt more protective fire building standards.

*Initiate controlled burns and make strategic cuts in adjacent forests to create a buffer between the fuel source and inhabited areas.

*Collect data on homes impacted by previous wildfires to better understand those building materials and practices which contributed to homes burning or not burning.

*Use flame resistant materials to retrofit existing infrastructure and for new building construction.

*Support local governments to motivate voluntary fire risk management practices, such as: 1) clearing fuel around structures (e.g., brush, leaves), 2) designating local safe zones that can provide shelter during fires, and 3) improving public communication regarding climate and extreme weather conditions that increase fire risk.

Irrespective of the effectiveness of these strategies, the growing threat of more frequent and severe wildfires will make it increasingly difficult to prevent such fires from occurring or controlling the impacts of those that ignite. The ultimate wildfire risk management strategy, therefore, is to shy away from building in areas prone to wildfire risk, and further consider whether it makes sense to replace structures that have fallen victim to a previous wildfire. This approach may not seem popular, particularly for established communities. However, the time has come to acknowledge that high-risk wildfire areas are becoming more widespread and combustible. If we fail to acknowledge this reality, don't be surprised if we get "burned".

If we fail to acknowledge this reality, don't be surprised if we get "burned".

The political will to acknowledge the threat of climate risk and to take meaningful action has not lived up to what is sorely needed. Instead, government officials continue to prioritize short-term economic incentives by authorizing development in areas known to be at high risk. Expensive infrastructure, such as roads and bridges, are maintained and rebuilt despite these risks, in denial that Mother Nature will strike again. And when she does, the rest of us are expected to foot the bill to excuse such poor decision-making and to enable the recurrence of similar outcomes in the future. As a nation, we are losing the appetite to provide a financial safety net for such risky behavior. And the insurance industry is losing interest in offering climate risk protection at affordable prices, if making it available at all.

Absent a government directive, the onus is on individuals, businesses and communities alike to invest in adaptation strategies designed to be resilient to the current and future onslaught of climate disasters. There is no one-size-fits-all playbook for risk management strategies, as each location faces different climate risks and has varying infrastructure, population demographics, resource availability and other considerations.

We are also learning that in some locations "adapt-in-place strategies" may not be sufficient. An emerging strategy for responding to climate risk in those instances is one that requires fundamentally and permanently changing human interactions with nature. Coined *managed retreat*, it involves relocating individuals or entire communities, their supporting infrastructure and services, and perhaps flora and fauna to another geographical area simply because it is no longer sensible or feasible to provide adequate protection at that location.

When, whether and how to relocate is the subject of much study nowadays. The issues are challenging, requiring a complex understanding of place attachment, the interconnectedness with other systems and people, and whether laws and regulations permit governments to authorize relocation. Relocation may also place additional stress on receiving communities, as the influx of new people puts greater demand on transportation, housing, employment, health care, energy and other critical infrastructure systems. Without proper planning, these so-called unintended consequences can create new risks that could offset the benefits of relocation.

Making an immediate and compelling effort to strengthen our management of climate risk is a necessity and no longer an option if we want our society to survive. We must come together to put much-needed resources into strengthening community and infrastructure resilience. We can choose to kick the can down the road or even exacerbate the situation by continuing to act in ways that fly in the face of risk-informed decision-making. But if we do, many will suffer needlessly and the gap between the climate threats we face and our ability to overcome them will only widen.

Grappling With Cybersecurity

While it emerged in the 1970s, the internet did not become visible to the general public until the early 1990s. As of 2020, however, approximately 4.5 billion people, or more than one-half of the world population, had access to the internet.

The internet has revolutionized communications and methods of commerce by enabling computers around the world to interconnect. We use the internet to share information via email, social media, and audio and video transmission. It provides businesses with a means for supporting sales and service without the overhead required in operating traditional brick and mortar facilities.

The existence and proliferation of the internet, however, has become a two-edged sword. For all of its benefits, the internet is also proving to be an effective tool for criminal activity and other cyber intrusions. In the discussion below, these activities have been organized into three threat categories: 1) cybercrime, 2) cyberespionage, and 3) cyberwarfare. Each threat brings unique characteristics that warrant special treatment.

The existence and proliferation of the internet, however, has become to be a two-edged sword.

Cybercrime is the domain of organized crime units. These cartels operate in a manner not all that different from drug trafficking. The objective is to steal money, often by accessing bank accounts and transferring funds to accounts that are set up to appear legitimate. With businesses increasingly dependent on electronic data and computer networks to conduct daily operations, growing pools of personal and financial information are being transferred and stored online. This can compromise our personal privacy, with financial institutions and other businesses exposed to potentially enormous liability with a data security breach.

The costs associated with cybercrime are increasing, with dollar losses in 2022 estimated at $10.3 billion, representing the highest annual amount since the U.S. Internet Crime Complaint Center began tracking cybercrime statistics two decades ago. Experts caution that the actual amount of fraudulent activity could be much higher, since many identity theft occurrences go unreported. The abuse has become so prevalent that companies are turning to a new cybersecurity strategy that assumes breaches already exist and must be rooted out.

It is quite likely that you, a family member or a friend has been a victim of cybercrime, where your identity has been compromised in some fashion. According to recent information published by the U.S. Cybersecurity and Infrastructure Security Agency, 47% of Americans have had their personal information exposed by cybersecurity criminals. It may have involved illegal use of your credit or debit card, someone creating a fake birth certificate, driver's license or Social Security card, or perhaps using your credentials when looking for a job or applying for benefits. Or maybe someone has opened an unauthorized utility account or applied for a loan in your name, created counterfeit checks, or filed a fraudulent tax return using your information. Another common intrusion is imposter scams, carried out by a perpetrator appearing to be a trusted organization or individual, who tricks a person into sending money to them.

Cybercrime techniques can vary, making it difficult to devise a one-size-fits-all approach to prevent these attacks. One popular technique is the use of malware, essentially a file or program designed to harm a computer user. Worms, viruses and trojans are terms commonly associated with malware. A worm self-replicates and distributes new versions of itself through the network it has intruded to other computers that share the same network. Viruses are software codes that are inserted within the code of another stand-alone program, then instruct the infected program to take malicious action. A trojan is a program that cannot reproduce itself but tricks the user into activating it in order to release its malicious behavior.

> Cybercrime techniques can vary, making it difficult to devise a one-size-fits-all approach to preventing these attacks.

Social engineering is another common technique, relying on human interaction to trick a user into breaking security procedures to gain sensitive information. Phishing is a form of social engineering where a fraudulent email or text message resembling a reputable source is sent randomly; spear phishing is a specialized form of phishing, targeted to a specific user. The attackers can also operate a man-in-the-middle scheme, whereby they intercept and relay messages between two parties who believe they are communicating with each other. Notably, cybercriminals are becoming less interested in stealing personal information directly from consumers, preferring to take advantage of poor consumer cyber hygiene to commit identity-related crimes against businesses using stolen credentials like logins and passwords.

A variety of well-known breaches has led to identity theft in the past decade. Two attacks on Yahoo, in 2013 and 2014, respectively, represented the largest data breaches in history at the time. The first attack exposed 3 billion user accounts, while the second one compromised 500 million accountholders. Hackers were able to obtain names, passwords, email addresses, telephone numbers, birthdates, and security questions and answers.

Some attacks have resulted in embarrassing and potentially tragic personal outcomes. Adult Friend Finder, an adult dating and pornography site, was breached in 2016, exposing 412 million user accounts, gaining access to email addresses, passwords, dates of last visit, browser information, IP addresses and site membership status. This followed a breach at the same site one year earlier, in which personal information was obtained and leaked by hackers, making known details of email addresses, usernames, birthdates, sexual preferences and whether users were seeking extramarital affairs.

Other attacks have lingered for prolonged periods of time prior to being discovered. In 2014, eBay's network was breached using credentials of three employees. Hackers maintained inside access for 229 days, collecting personal information on 145 million users. More remarkable was the multi-year attack on Marriott International, which began in 2014 and lasted until 2018, enabling hackers to obtain contact information, passport numbers, preferred guest records and credit card numbers of 500 million customers.

Among the more ironic data breaches occurred when Equifax fell victim. As one of the three largest consumer credit reporting agencies along with Experian and TransUnion, Equifax collects and aggregates information on over 800 million individual consumers and more than 88 million businesses worldwide. Consequently, one would think that of all enterprises, the company would adhere to the strictest cybersecurity protocols since it would be one of the most desirable targets on the planet for a hacker to breach. Yet, in 2017, this occurred, compromising the personal information of 148 million consumers, including Social Security numbers, birth dates, addresses, driver license numbers and credit card information.

High-profile data breaches continue to this day to threaten businesses and consumers alike. In 2019, large-scale data breaches were experienced by Capital One Financial Corporation that exposed 100 million accounts and Adobe Creative Cloud that exposed approximately 7 million users. MGM Resorts was hit by a 2020 data breach that exposed the personal information of more than 10 million guests, while another breach at Marriott Hotels that same year reached a data system containing the personal information of over 5 million customers. In January of 2021, more than 280 million Microsoft customer records were left unprotected. Over the past couple of years, this disturbing trend has continued, with several large-scale breaches of well-known enterprises included in the list.

Cyberespionage is a type of cyberattack whereby an unauthorized user attempts to access security-sensitive information or intellectual property for competitive advantage or political reasons. With several nations implicated as major players in promoting this form of illegal activity, cyberespionage is considered a growing security threat. Moreover, most criminals remain at large due to a lack of extradition agreements between countries, and difficulty enforcing international law.

Common cyberespionage targets include large corporations, government agencies, academic institutions, think tanks, and other organizations considered to have strategic value. Targeted campaigns can also be waged against individuals, such as prominent political leaders, government officials, business executives and celebrities. Depending on the perpetrator's objective, the information they collect can be retained for subsequent malicious use or wiped out so the victim no longer has access to that information.

Most cyberespionage activity is characterized by a sophisticated, sustained cyberattack in which the intruder establishes an undetected presence in a network in order to reside for a prolonged period of time to intercept sensitive data. Adversaries are typically well-funded, experienced teams of cybercriminals who spend significant time and resources identifying and exploiting vulnerabilities of the target organization or individual.

The entry point for planting malicious software is often made by accessing the network through a particular individual's credentials. This is often done by tricking victims into providing personal information by encouraging them to click malicious links or download malware. One approach involves perpetrators infecting legitimate websites commonly visited by the victim with malware. Another approach targets a specific individual with fraudulent emails or text messages in order to steal login credentials or other sensitive information. Inside actors are also utilized, whose objective is to convince an employee or contractor to share system access to unauthorized users.

Notable cases of cyberespionage include research efforts related to the COVID-19 pandemic. Since April 2020, intrusion activity targeting coronavirus research laboratories has been reported against the U.S., United Kingdom, Spain, South Korea, Japan and Australia. Another cyberespionage attack was attributed to Fancy Bear, a Russia-based group targeting U.S. political and European military organizations. Emails were used purporting to be from reputable companies, inducing individuals to reveal personal information to spoofed websites that closely resemble legitimate ones in order to gain access. Goblin Panda, a China-based cyber espionage group, has utilized Microsoft Word as an entry point to target defense, energy and government sectors in Southeast Asia, particularly Vietnam. Finally, Helix Kitten, suspected to be Iran-based, has targeted organizations in aerospace, energy, financial, government, hospitality and telecommunications by sending phishing messages that appear highly relevant to targeted personnel.

More recently, SolarWinds, a major U.S. information technology firm, was the subject of a cyberattack that spread to its clients and went undetected for nearly a year. Foreign hackers, believed to be residing in Russia, were able to use the hack to spy on Fortune 500 companies and other elite organizations, as well as upper echelons of the U.S. government. Hackers accomplished this intrusion by secretly breaking into SolarWinds' software system and adding a malicious code to create backdoor access to Orion, the company's software product. Orion is widely used by companies to manage their information technology, including SolarWinds' 33,000 customers. Beginning as early as March of 2020, SolarWinds unwittingly sent out software updates to its customers that included the hacked code, enabling the hackers to install additional malware to help them spy on numerous companies and organizations.

The growing sophistication of cyberespionage actors has enabled them to bypass many standard cybersecurity products and legacy systems. In response, a variety of cybersecurity and intelligence solutions have been developed to assist potential targets in better understanding their threat adversaries and attack techniques. Sensor capabilities are also being deployed that provide broader visibility across an organization's computing environment, with the goal of detecting when and where an unsuccessful attack or successful intrusion may have occurred. Additionally, access to threat intelligence reports has helped targeted organizations more easily recognize potential threat actors and the weapons being used.

Arguably the most dangerous form of cyber vulnerability is *cyberwarfare*. This relatively new threat utilizes the internet to transmit malware that instructs software control systems to malfunction in ways that cause cyber or physical harm. Attacks can be directed at destroying, interfering with, corrupting, monitoring, or otherwise damaging software operating the system.

> **Arguably the most dangerous form of cyber insecurity is cyberwarfare.**

One particular type of cyber weapon is distributed denial-of-service (DDoS). Attackers use malware to hijack a computer network, flooding the target with demands, thereby slowing legitimate traffic or crashing the system altogether. Early application of this method involved cyberattacks waged against the countries of Estonia in 2007 and Georgia in 2008. On both occasions, it is alleged that Russian hackers conducted DDoS attacks against key government, financial, media, and commercial websites. These attacks temporarily denied access by the governments and citizens to key sources of information and communications.

A well-known case of cyberwarfare is the Stuxnet virus, discovered in 2010, whose purpose was not just to infect a computer system, but to cause real-world physical effects. Stuxnet was designed to target centrifuges used to produce the enriched uranium that powers nuclear weapons and reactors. Once inside, the virus alters the computer's programming, prompting the centrifuges to spin too quickly and for too long, damaging or destroying the equipment in the process. While this is happening, the computer is led to believe that everything is working fine, making it difficult to detect or diagnose what is going wrong until it is too late. Stuxnet was used to penetrate an Iranian nuclear facility and manipulate the software control system to spin centrifuges being used to create nuclear fuel at rates that caused them to burst. The attack, purported to be a U.S. and Israeli initiative, delayed Iran's nuclear program for several years.

Russia's cyber involvement in the 2016 U.S. presidential election is considered by many as a form of cyberwarfare. A suspected motive of Russian President Vladimir Putin was to discredit candidate Hillary Clinton, blaming her for inciting mass protests against his regime. Russian hackers penetrated the computer systems of the Democratic National Committee, obtaining emails, chats and opposition research. This information was made public via WikiLeaks, a web site run by an organization that specializes in making available large datasets of censored or otherwise restricted official materials. Information published via WikiLeaks continued until Election Day, a race that Clinton lost in what the pundits considered to be an upset.

Surfacing more recently on the cyberwarfare landscape is ransomware. This involves the use of malware designed to encrypt files on a device, rendering them and the systems that rely on them unusable. The perpetrators then demand a ransom in exchange for decryption, with a commitment not to sell or leak sensitive information if the ransom is paid.

Ransomware attacks are growing at a disturbing rate. In 2019, the number of ransomware incursions more than doubled from the previous year, to the point where, worldwide, an organization fell victim to a ransomware attack every 14 seconds on average. This upward trend is continuing; notably the U.S. Cybersecurity and Infrastructure Security Agency reported in early 2022 that it was aware of ransomware incidents that had been perpetrated against 14 of the 16 U.S. critical infrastructure sectors. Although more organizations are now purchasing insurance to protect against this risk, ransom demands are growing larger as attackers realize that companies can meet higher monetary ultimatums.

The use of ransomware gained prominence as a result of the WannaCry attack, which occurred in 2017. Purported to be carried out by North Korea, the attack targeted computers running Microsoft Windows operating systems via a type of malware that encrypts data, preventing systems from accessing their own information. This malware also spread copies of itself from computer-to-computer without any human interaction, dramatically expanding its reach; within four days, 200,000 computers in 150 countries had been affected. A ransom, paid in cryptocurrency, was demanded by the hackers in order to release the encryption. Fortunately, the attack was halted rather quickly through emergency patches released by Microsoft and the discovery of a kill switch within the malware code that prevented infected computers from further spreading WannaCry.

In the Spring of 2021, hackers successfully targeted the Colonial Pipeline, the largest fuel pipeline in the U.S. Entry into Colonial's system was the result of a single compromised password among employees who could remotely access the company's computer network. Ironically, the account was no longer in use at the time of the attack, but remained active as a source of network access. Because system access was not protected by requiring multifactor authentication, the hackers were able to breach the Colonial network by using just a compromised username and password. The perpetrators stole nearly 100 gigabytes of data, threatening to leak the information unless a ransom payment in the form of cryptocurrency was made. Colonial immediately shut down its fuel pipeline, representing the first time the company had closed the entire operation in its 57-year history. With Colonial responsible for transporting roughly 2.5 million barrels of fuel daily from Texas to the Northeast, which represents 45% of all fuel consumed on the East Coast, the outage led to long lines at gas stations, many of which ran out, and higher fuel prices. Colonial paid the hackers, an affiliate of a Russia-linked cybercrime group known as DarkSide, a $4.4 million ransom, $2.3 million of which the FBI was able to track and recover.

Just a few weeks later, JBS, the world's largest meat processor, suffered a ransomware attack that targeted servers powering its software systems in Australia and North America. The company responded by shutting down its U.S. beef plants and introducing operating delays at its pork plants. The attack was attributed to REvil, a Russian-based group reputed to be one of the most prolific ransomware organizations. JBS paid an $11 million ransom in Bitcoin to the hackers, allowing the company to resume its operations within four days from when it first learned of the intrusion.

What is particularly concerning about cyberwarfare is the number of critical infrastructure facilities that are managed by software control systems, and the fact that such sites can be rendered inoperable without putting armed forces at risk. When combined with the growing sophistication of cyber hackers, it raises the possibility for a coordinated and advanced attack that could disrupt any number of modern-day services, including utility operations, health care, financial markets and major elections, among others.

What is particularly concerning about cyberwarfare is the number of critical infrastructure facilities that are managed by software control systems...

While cyberwarfare by itself can cause harm to critical infrastructure, it can also act as a precursor to a more conventional attack. It is not a far reach, for example, for a cyberattack to render a communication system inoperable, following which a physical attack would commence, giving the enemy considerable advantage by disrupting a timely and coordinated response by the opponent.

Arguably the greatest challenge in defending against

cyberattacks is the low cost of entry into cyberspace and the ease with which anyone using the right tools can mask their identity, location and motive. This makes it extremely difficult for targets of these attacks to deter or respond to the perpetrator.

As a result, defending against cyberwarfare has become a priority for the public and private sector. Key features of a major cyber defense structure include firewalls to filter network traffic, data encryption, tools to prevent and detect network intruders, physical security of equipment and facilities, and training and monitoring of network users. Given the seriousness and specialized nature of this threat, a growing number of defense agencies are creating organizational units specifically tasked to thwart the escalating threat of cyberwarfare.

There is no question that the advent of the internet has had a significant impact on our lives. Accessing and sending a trove of information in real-time from virtually anywhere has motivated the use of this method for a variety of business and social purposes. However, while these benefits are being realized, they are coming at the price of worrisome consequences in the form of cyber insecurity. The combined threats of cybercrime, cyberespionage and cyberwarfare leaves much to be reckoned with.

The success of cybersecurity rests on individuals and organizations to consistently and uniformly adopt best practice risk management strategies. These include:

- Using multifactor authentication – Require a user to present at least two pieces of evidence, delivered independently, to verify the validity of their identity when logging into an account. One common form of multifactor authentication is for the user to enter their username and password, following which they receive a cell phone text message with a number that must be correctly entered before account access is permitted.

- Utilizing a password manager – Store passwords in an encrypted format and provides secure access to all the password information through the use of a master password.
- Implementing a firewall – Monitor incoming and outgoing network traffic, and determine whether to allow or block specific traffic based on a defined set of security rules.
- Documenting cybersecurity policies – Standards of behavior that involve computer use, such as password sharing, avoiding malicious web sites and attachments, steering clear of unapproved cloud applications, and encrypting sensitive files.
- Taking comprehensive cybersecurity training – Understand vulnerabilities and threats to cyber operations, including personal responsibilities and accountability when using a computer, particularly when it is part of a larger network.
- Utilizing safe password practices – Recommendations as to character length and type, as well as proper use of password dictionaries, managers and generators.
- Regularly backing up data – Insure against the loss of valuable data by copying and storing the data in multiple independent locations (e.g., external hard drive, cloud backup service) in case the original source is corrupted.
- Installing and updating anti-malware software – Programs that scan a computer to detect and remove threats when malware is found.
- Having a security plan for mobile devices – Treat cybersecurity on mobile devices no differently than the protections afforded to desktop computers.

Despite these efforts, there are no assurances that hackers will be successfully repelled. For individual abuses, it is important to monitor personal information to discover problems quickly.

This is best accomplished by checking financial accounts and statements frequently, and reviewing credit reports on a regular basis. If your identity has been compromised, immediately contact the business where the intrusion has occurred to report a fraudulent activity and to dispute any unauthorized transactions. In addition, file an Identity Theft Report to the Federal Trade Commission at IdentityTheft.gov. The Identity Theft Report can be used to permanently block fraudulent information from appearing on your credit report, prevent a company from continuing to collect debts that result from identity theft, and can be used to place an extended fraud alert on your credit report.

There are ominous signs that the future of cybersecurity could be as or more problematic. For one, the increase in globalization and lack of cyber borders creates an environment where malicious actors can operate anywhere in the world and likely immune from prosecution. Moreover, new information gathering techniques are constantly under development by those desiring to exploit unsuspecting victims.

There are ominous signs that the future of cybersecurity could be as or more problematic.

While cyber attackers must overcome cyber defenses, the offense holds a dominant position because any defense must contend with attacks on large networks that are inherently vulnerable and run by fallible human users. In order to be effective in a cyberattack, the perpetrator has to succeed only once, whereas the defender must be successful every single time.

Avoiding the Dark Side of Social Networking

Facebook, YouTube, WhatsApp, Instagram, WeChat and Tik Tok are social networks estimated to each have more than one billion users. With such a global presence, the phenomenon of social networking is clearly changing the cultural landscape for both individuals and businesses. How much of this is a good thing? And what are the risks associated with perpetrators of social networking or innocent posts that lead to unfortunate outcomes? It begs the question of which way the pendulum is swinging.

There are clear advantages to being active on social media. We do this to maintain existing relationships and to make new ones. These connections not only inform family and friends of what we are doing, but also represent an effective way to organize events, share pictures, and converse on topics of mutual interest. With social networking able to leverage global positioning system (GPS) technology, contacts are also aware of our location at any given time. Moreover, we can customize our information sources by choosing to follow whoever and whatever we wish.

Businesses too are engaging in social networking, using it to connect with existing customers, create brand awareness, expand reach, sell products and services, improve reputation, recruit employees, and stay abreast of the competition. Some businesses rely heavily, if not exclusively, on social networks and the data mining that comes with it. Additionally, these platforms create business opportunities for entrepreneurs and start-ups who may otherwise experience barriers to entry for economic or other reasons. The mere existence of a social media workforce contributes to a more vibrant economy.

Law enforcement agencies use social media to help identify, catch and prosecute criminals. A recent survey by the International Association of Chiefs of Police found that virtually all police departments use social media to help solve crimes. Social media also allows for rapid dissemination of public health and safety information, under both normal circumstances and during crises. Moreover, emergency managers can utilize social networking to help locate, in real-time, those in need and the response resources required.

Many educators believe social networking helps students perform better in school to foster learning by being able to share content, discuss educational topics and communicate interactively about assignments. Social media also offers greater access to educational resources, especially important in lifting up vulnerable populations.

Political and social causes have also benefitted from using social networks to promote grassroots efforts. These platforms provide opportunities for promoting change, including helping to disarm stigmas. Activists are able to leverage a rapid, no-cost method to organize, disseminate information, and mobilize followers. Social networking is also well-suited for crowdsourcing and crowdfunding, allowing a larger populous to collectively accomplish a stated goal.

These social connections can also improve our quality of life and reduce the risk of health problems, particularly for those who are socially isolated or introverted. This can be especially true for senior citizens, whose connections with a social group have been associated with improvements in mental health, stroke recovery and memory retention. More generally, friends and family on social media can promote healthy lifestyle habits and offer moral support in difficult times.

Finally, social networking can just plain serve as a source of personal enjoyment. It can be a break from a mundane activity or as a form of relaxation. Moreover, it can be entertaining to notice comments and likes showing up on posts, or to learn what friends and family are doing without having to ask them directly.

There is, however, a growing dark side of social networking. With vast amounts of information being shared online, much of it out of our control and potentially damning, issues over privacy are a significant and growing concern. Sharing too much about ourselves in public can create a litany of problems, as once a post is out there, it may last into perpetuity, even if the originator deletes it from their own account. Messages or pictures tied to our social network activity or those posted by friends and associates create opportunities for predators and others interested in scrutinizing our behavior to enter our lives in undesirable ways.

Businesses are finding the going can be tough as well. Opportunities exist for a disgruntled employee or customer, or even a prankster, to lodge a scathing review of the organization's performance, knowing that the more prolific the commentary, the more likely the negative information will go viral.

Another danger involves how much we rely on social networking as a primary source for news and other information. We can easily end up in a filter bubble, either by accident or by choice, isolating ourselves from new information or being able to engage with people who have different perspectives. And if you happen to be in a bubble filled with dangerous misinformation and unsavory characters, it can lead to serious personal repercussions. Examples include immoral behavior, such as easy access to pornography involving minors, or radical behavior, such as participating in socially-network organized insurrections.

Using social media may also harm our existing reputation or future prospects. Employers, college administrators and others are known to routinely scan social networks, looking for profiles, tweets, photos, videos or other information that could provide evidence of illegal or unethical behavior.

Dangerous habits can also form that put lives at risk. Interacting on smartphones while driving creates distractions that can cause aberrant driver behavior, leading to harmful accidents. More innocuous, but certainly annoying, is difficulty to gain or retain someone's full attention during a conversation because they are constantly browsing social media. These distractions can extend to situations in which a heavy commitment to social network use leads to chronic procrastination in performing tasks or responsibilities, or produces sedentary lifestyle habits. Staring into the artificial light from a computer or phone screen at night has also been identified as an inhibitor to getting a proper night's sleep.

For those of us struggling to fit in with peers, particularly teens and young adults, the pressure to be accepted and liked by everyone posting on social media, or the fear of being a cyberbullied, can manifest stress, anxiety and even depression. Studies have shown that social networking can promote anti-social behavior, leading to feelings of isolation. By being able to connect whenever we want by a simple tap on the smartphone or click of a mouse, online interaction has become a dominant substitute for face-to-face interaction.

Even the educational benefits of social networking are being challenged. Children who spend over three hours engaged in social networking on a normal school day reportedly suffer from mental health difficulties. It has also been asserted that students who use social networking sites while studying score lower on tests and post lower grade point averages. Moreover, social networking can provide an avenue for cheating on school assignments.

Finally, social media sites may not scan messages for viruses or phishing scams, creating an open door for hackers to steal our identity or plant malware with nefarious intent.

A topic in its own right, but closely tied to social networking, is the emergence of artifical intelligence. AI algorithms locate and process large amounts of information and data, translating it into usable form. This creates opportunities to streamline preparation of documents and narratives, saving time and energy.

AI is used to obtain real-time answers to questions, engage in personalized conversation and deliver customized content based on expressed interests. It can also help with brainstorming, understanding difficult concepts, writing computer code, and a variety of other purposes.

However, the benefits of such a powerful tool come at a price. Notably, AI operates by having bots scrape relevant information and data from a broad range of sources utilizing the internet, often without discern for the source or whether the information is factual or unbiased. Moreover, these bots lack human emotional ability in determining the social impact of what is being collected and shared. This creates an avenue for AI output to contain falsehoods and biases that many of us believe to be objective information with an understanding of emotional ramifications.

Another consideration involves data privacy. Since AI is scraping information from multiple sources and is also trained to recognize patterns, it can be used to gather data on people without direct access to personal information.

These limitations to incorporate ethics and morality are recognized to some extent by the AI industry. Efforts are afoot to enable bots while scaping data to find and filter out spam, guideline-breaking or inappropriate content, including banning those accounts that post such content. Instagram, for example, is known to use AI with this objective in mind.

Social networking experts are also concerned about the impact of AI use on personal work habits. Studies have found increased laziness and carelessness as well as decline in work quality when humans work alongside AI robots. Such cultural loafing also tends to retard human creativity required to engage in problem-solving and decisionmaking.

Development of strategies for managing AI risk is in its infancy given the rapid emergence of this technology in such a short period of time. Bill Gates believes that this will require a collaborative effort among governments, political leaders, businesses and the public at large.

Development of strategies for managing AI risk is in its infancy given the rapid emergence of this technology in such a short period of time.

Governments and political leaders will need to enact laws and regulations that effectively address issues related to use of misinformation, digital alteration of images, invasion of privacy, and compromised learning methods, among others. AI developers and businesses making extensive use of AI must place ethical and moral principles at the top of their priority list in developing and deploying AI systems, including notification of when AI is being used instead of interacting with a human. Finally, the public at large should stay abreast of the evolution of AI, its uses and abuses, while also participating in an ongoing, constructive discussion on how to ensure that the benefits outweigh the risks when all is said and done.

◆ ◆ ◆

One type of social networking warrants its own conversation: cyber activism.

Cyber activism involves the use of internet-based socializing and communication techniques to promote a specific motive or cause. Because of the ease and low cost of entry, virtually any individual or organization can utilize social networks to raise awareness, gather followers and broadcast messages to advance a specific motive or cause. This has proven to be a valuable tool for activist movements, whose dependence on social networking is expected to grow in the future.

One of the most popular examples of cyber activism is the Ice Bucket Challenge, which began in 2014 as a campaign to grow awareness and raise money for ALS (Amyotrophic Lateral Sclerosis) research. Spread rapidly on Facebook, posts often consisted of a video showing a participant completing the challenge by dumping a bucket of ice water on their head, and then nominating others to either complete the challenge and post their own video as proof, or donate $100 to the ALS Association to support research for the disease. According to the Association, this campaign has raised over $115 million since the challenge began.

Another form of cyber activism involves environmental protection. Greenpeace created Greenwire, a social media network for environmental activists to interact online. By forming a community and having meaningful online conversations, Greenwire serves as a source for motivating activists to develop policies that promote environmental preservation via civic engagement, civil disobedience and other mechanisms. It also creates a venue to connect supporter and cause, which in turn encourages more people to make financial contributions in support of environmental initiatives.

Black Lives Matter has also benefitted immensely from the use of cyber activism. It began as a grassroots movement calling for wider consciousness of anti-black racism and police violence based on a Facebook message posted by Alicia Garza, an activist from Oakland, CA in July 2013. After watching a Florida jury decline to convict George Zimmerman for the death of unarmed teen Trayvon Martin, Ms. Garza posted her thoughts on the impact of the verdict, ending her message with "Black people. I love you. I love us. Our lives matter." Garza's friend, Patrisse Cullors, a community organizer who worked on prison reform issues, read the post and began sharing it, using the hashtag #blacklivesmatter. The slogan exploded into popular consciousness the following year, with the death of 18-year-old Michael Brown, who was fatally shot by a white police officer in Ferguson, MO. The Black Lives Matter movement has continued to grow since then, and has an influential global reach today.

After the Parkland, FL mass shooting at Marjory Stoneman Douglas High School in 2018, #MarchForOurLives was born. Students created this hashtag to protest the need for gun control in the U.S. This launched a movement of hundreds of protests across the country, including one in Washington, D.C. attended by an estimated 200,000 people. Similarly, the Arab Spring, a 2011 series of pro-democracy uprisings of several largely Muslim countries, relied on social media as a key communication tool for activists to organize in the wake of fast-changing protests.

White nationalists have seized social networking as a platform to effectively disseminate their message to a mass audience. This group has achieved success in exploiting human vulnerabilities to quickly and efficiently promote their ideologies, including the use of strategic domain names and hidden propaganda content. The white nationalist movement has also leveraged social platform algorithms that tend to work in a self-reinforcing manner, essentially connecting communities of like-minded people, thereby reinforcing the psychological effects of confirmation bias.

Corporations, too, are using cyber activism to increase support for their causes in addition to promoting business interests. Walmart has taken an active stance in urging lawmakers to enact stricter gun control measures. Amazon, Apple, Coca-Cola, Facebook, Nike and Uber have teamed up with advocacy organizations focused on racial equality and criminal justice reform. The past decade has also witnessed corporate activism supporting LGBTQ rights and immigration. However, the success of corporate cyber activism has been diminished by the emergence of a cancel culture movement aimed at specific businesses for their stance on these issues.

Finally, social networking has been an important vehicle for raising awareness of sexual assault. It has provided an outlet for victims to be comfortable sharing experiences without feeling a sense of blame or guilt. For example, the #notguilty movement was formed in 2015 when an Oxford University student shared a "letter to her attacker", describing how she was sexually assaulted and how she chose to respond and build from that point in her life. At the end of the letter, she urged readers to send a letter back describing their own sexual assault experience with the hashtag #notguilty. This cyber activism brought global attention and inspired many to share their stories.

The #MeToo movement represents another powerful example of cyber activism against sexual assault. Initially focused on exposing the extent of sexual assault suffered by Hollywood actors, the movement soon spread to include all forms of sexual assault, particularly in the workplace. The extended reach of the #MeToo movement is prompting dramatic cultural change among employers.

◆ ◆ ◆

We are embroiled in a Catch-22 whereby leveraging social networking to our advantage simultaneously exposes us to potential abuse. Social networking has become an obsession and as we continue to spend large amounts of time engaged in this activity, we are becoming addicted to its trappings. Doing so has affected our social landscape in a profound way, creating one of the more confounding risk management dilemmas that we, as individuals and organizations, face today.

> Social networking has become an obsession...
> we are becoming addicted to its trappings.

By making heavy use of social networking sites, we are placing ourselves at risk of being captured in electronic memory for the entire world to see. While generally playful and innocent, the repercussions of many postings can be harsh or even cruel. A casual party scene can lead to termination of an employee or cause a prospective employer to reject an applicant's candidacy. Videos of extramarital trysts can fracture families. Cyber bullying can leave one emotionally damaged. In some cases, individuals have felt so exposed and shamed that they have taken their own lives from a discovery having been made public.

How do we navigate the minefield that social networking presents? At what point does our risk appetite accept that there is no perfect solution to this conundrum? Such questions come down to our assessment of whether the rewards gained by social networking are worth the risks, and if so, how we can reduce the risks such that rewards dominate the tradeoff. This is not just a problem reserved for the rich, famous and powerful; they are the very same questions being asked by all of us.

> At what point does our risk appetite accept that there is no perfect solution to the social networking conundrum?

Sure, there are ways to protect one's privacy by restricting access to only those contacts who you approve. Yet this is becoming increasingly difficult to control given the number of combinations of friend's friends and the level of communication activity. Of utmost concern is the lack of control over this environment for impressionable children and young adults, who often deny access to parents and other responsible adults who might otherwise provide advice and guidance.

In the face of this dilemma, it is time to re-evaluate how we manage social networking risk. In the past, we may have had reasonable control over the transparency of our actions. Now, the pendulum has swung decidedly in the opposite direction. From a risk management perspective, we should assume that anything we do will be accessible through some form of electronic media. Knowing this, we have a choice to make. We can either elect to not participate in a manner that we may regret, accept that our actions will be in full public view, or make a concerted effort to keep these "leaks" from occurring.

Employing a leak-proof strategy is not that easy, however. What has come with the electronic information explosion are numerous avenues for leaks to occur, both accidental and intentional. To protect ourselves, we must account for the unintended consequences associated with making seemingly innocent posts of activities and opinions on a social networking site. This will hopefully guard against irresponsible or hateful behaviors of "friends" and from malicious attempts by cyber activists intent on feeding propaganda to influence our beliefs and actions. It speaks to the need for teaching smart social networking for all age groups.

So, have we reached George Orwell's vision of Big Brother? Oddly enough, Orwell was fixated on an authority spying on each of us. We have created a new breed of animal – us spying on each other.

We have created a new breed of animal – us spying on each other.

Combatting Infectious Diseases

Caused by microorganisms – bacteria, viruses, parasites and fungi – infectious diseases can spread, directly or indirectly, from one person to another. Infectious diseases can also originate in animals, be transmitted to humans, and then transmitted between humans.

While some infectious diseases are localized and spread in a limited manner, often with little or no mortality, health officials become more alarmed when these diseases emerge with greater impact. When this occurs, these breakouts are considered endemics, epidemics or pandemics, depending on scale. An *endemic* is an infectious disease that typically afflicts a specific population or region. When a disease spreads rapidly to a large number of people in a given population over a short period of time, it is considered an *epidemic*. A *pandemic* differs from an epidemic in that it affects a wider geographical area, often worldwide, infects a larger number of people, is highly transmissible, and has a more significant impact on human casualties and societal disruption.

Infectious diseases are not a new phenomenon. They have been a part of human life since the beginning of mankind. History abounds of notable infectious diseases that caused considerable human suffering and threatened massive population loss, some recorded far back in time. For example, the Bubonic Plague, also known as Black Death, occurred for nearly a decade in the mid-fourteenth century, a pandemic that covered Asia and Europe. It is estimated that 20 million Europeans died from this disease, one-third of the continent's population. Sadly, livestock were also susceptible to the disease, decimating many herds and flocks. Although the Bubonic Plague had run its course by the early 1350s, it has not been completely eradicated. Despite modern sanitation, public health practices and antibiotics that have greatly mitigated the impact of this disease, a few thousand worldwide cases are still reported every year.

Infectious diseases are not a new phenomenon. They have been part of human life since the beginning of mankind.

Another well-known pandemic, the Spanish Flu, occurred during the period of 1918-1920, with impacts felt globally. The disease, whose origin remains unknown, infected humans in the form of the H1N1 virus. Coinciding with World War I, the Spanish Flu was able to spread rapidly through military camps, causing such carnage that more U.S. soldiers died from the virus than were killed in battle. With no vaccine for protection or antibiotics to treat secondary bacterial infections, control efforts were limited to isolation, quarantine, good personal hygiene, use of disinfectants and limitations on public gatherings. It is estimated that roughly 500 million people, approximately one-third of the world population at the time, contracted the disease, resulting in at least 50 million fatalities. The pandemic waned when a sufficient number of people who contracted the virus developed so-called herd immunity, with life returning to normal by the early 1920s.

This strand of flu did not disappear completely, however. Since then, the influenza virus has continuously mutated, passing through humans, pigs and other mammals. While today the 1918 H1N1 virus has morphed into just another seasonal flu, the strand's descendants comprise the influenza viruses we deal with today.

Fast forwarding to more recent times brings us to the H1N1 Swine Flu pandemic, which reached its peak in 2009 and 2010. This new strain of H1N1 was discovered in Mexico, believed to have been transmitted by pigs, hence the name. Although the impacts were felt worldwide, the U.S. was particularly hard hit. Highly contagious, the disease spread via saliva and mucus particles, magnified by actions such as sneezing and coughing, or by contact with a germ-covered surface and then touching one's eyes or nose. For these reasons, children and young adults were particularly vulnerable to disease transmission. The global impact: over 1.4 billion people infected, resulting in estimates ranging from 150,000 to 575,000 fatalities.

HIV (Human Immunodeficiency Virus)/AIDS (Acquired Immunodeficiency Syndrome) is a well-known pandemic that began in the early 1980's and remains potent today. Believed to have originated from a chimpanzee virus in Central Africa, this disease has caused at least 35 million deaths worldwide, representing the second leading cause of death in developing nations. HIV is most commonly transmitted through anal or vaginal sex, or from sharing needles, syringes or other drug injection equipment. If left untreated, it can lead to AIDS, the most severe phase of HIV infection. AIDS afflicts the immune system, causing such damage that one becomes highly vulnerable to contracting a variety of severe illnesses. There is currently no effective cure once people contract HIV, but with proper medical care the virus can be controlled.

While epidemics do not occur on as large a geographic scale as pandemics, they can prove lethal nonetheless to smaller populations. Well-known in U.S. history is the polio epidemic, with separate significant outbreaks occurring in 1916 and 1952, New York City being at the epicenter. Polio is a viral disease that affects the nervous system, spread through contact between people by nasal and oral secretions, and by contact with contaminated feces. Though most people recovered rapidly from polio, some suffered temporary or permanent paralysis and even death. President Franklin D. Roosevelt was among those whose bout with polio left him permanently paralyzed from the waist down. In 1955, Dr. Jonas Salk's polio vaccine was approved and quickly adopted throughout the world. By the mid-1990s, polio was eliminated from the Western Hemisphere, although it continues to circulate in Afghanistan and Pakistan, with occasional spread to neighboring countries.

Communities in western and central Africa were victims of a more recent epidemic, Ebola, particularly during the period from 2014 to 2016. Transmitted to humans from bats, Ebola is a deadly virus whose symptoms include fever, body aches and diarrhea. As the virus spreads through the body, it damages the immune system and vital organs, ultimately leading to severe, uncontrollable bleeding, killing up to 90% of people who contract the disease. Ebola spreads by contact with the skin or bodily fluids of an infected person, placing at high risk those who care for a sick Ebola patient, bury someone who has died from the disease, or touch contaminated needles or surfaces. Fortunately, one cannot contract Ebola from air, water or food, and a person who has Ebola but is asymptomatic cannot spread the disease.

Note that the prior review represents just a snapshot of the breadth and depth of infectious diseases, and does not provide a complete history of endemics, epidemics or pandemics that society has faced, even recently. Excluded from this discussion are diseases such as smallpox, scarlet fever, severe acute respiratory syndrome (SARS), meningitis, cholera, yellow fever, and Zika, among others.

Which brings us to COVID-19, an infectious disease caused by a coronavirus that likely emerged in the Wuhan region of China, although unclear whether it originated through animal transfer to humans or manifested in a scientific laboratory. A lengthy pandemic that continues to exist at the time of this writing, COVID-19 at times has ground life as we know it to a complete halt, leaving death and destruction along the way. And the disease has mutated several times, including highly transmissible and lethal Delta and Omicron variants.

While most people infected with COVID-19 experience mild to moderate respiratory illness and recover without requiring special treatment, older people and those with pre-existing conditions (cardiovascular disease, diabetes, chronic respiratory disease, cancer) are more likely to develop serious illness. Although the most common symptoms are fever, cough and fatigue, people suffering from severe COVID-19 cases often experience shortness of breath, loss of appetite, confusion, high temperature, and persistent pain or pressure in the chest. Complications leading to death can be due to respiratory failure, sepsis and septic shock, blood clots, or multi-organ failure. According to the World Health Organization, to date there have been over 765 million confirmed COVID-19 cases, resulting in nearly 7 million fatalities worldwide.

Some people who have had COVID-19, whether hospitalized or not, continue to experience effects over a lengthy period of time, a condition known as long-COVID. Common lingering symptoms include fatigue, shortness of breath or difficulty breathing, fever, headache, cough, chest or joint/muscle pain, memory loss, concentration or sleep problems, fast or pounding heartbeat, loss of taste or smell, depression or anxiety, and dizziness when standing up. These symptoms often become more pronounced after intense physical or mental activity.

Lost among the impacts of the outbreaks of serious infectious diseases and how they proliferate is the effect they can have on the economic, social and political fabric of our society. The COVID-19 pandemic provides vivid proof of the extent.

> Lost among the impacts of the outbreaks of serious infectious diseases… is the effect they have on the economic, social and political fabric of our society.

Let's begin with economics. Once it became clear that COVID-19 was out of control, people stayed home and businesses shut down. The hospitality and other service industries in particular, without any patrons, saw cash flow dwindle and reserves evaporate, resulting in large numbers of laid off workers. The curtailed need for supplies and other products normally consumed by these industries percolated through other business sectors who rely on delivering these goods. This tailspin created a financial crisis that required multiple government rescue packages in order to sustain economic survival. To make matters worse, the surge in demand for health care supplies and equipment, as well as purified water, household disinfectants and toiletries, could not be met by provisioners. The supply chain was also obstructed by the lack of workers available to produce and transport goods due to illness or fear of being exposed to virus transmission. Further exacerbating this problem was the business practice of many companies to maintain limited on-site inventory, a strategy to reduce operating costs in order to remain competitive in a global market; hence the surplus to draw from in-house was negligible.

The social aspects of the COVID-19 pandemic fared no better. With schools closed for extended periods of time, children were forced to stay at home and in need of a caretaker. Often this involved a parent or another family member taking primary responsibility for ensuring children were learning remotely and using the remainder of their time in meaningful and non-destructive ways. In some cases, this resulted in the primary caretaker leaving a steady job, while in other cases it required a radical change in living arrangements so that family members could work productively from home without these distractions.

Moreover, many important quality-of-life activities and events had to be canceled or deferred, such as dental visits, elective surgery, sporting events and recreational travel, in addition to weddings, reunions and other traditional gatherings.

Being cooped up at home, and often with less economic means, also created a more stressful environment. Not having social outlets – visiting friends, attending religious services, dining out, going to museums, etc. – led to more instances of depression, anxiety and other mental health conditions.

Most surprising, and deeply disturbing, has been the politicization of COVID-19. One would think that a virus which threatens the health of young and old, rich and poor, and all genders, races and ethnicities, would create a united front and an all-hands-on-deck commitment to fighting the disease. Yet, it instead became a polarizing event, pitting different factions against one another, resulting in a disjointed effort to detect COVID-19 victims, and to trace and track those who might have been exposed to an infected person. This created an aura of hostility and finger-pointing, as well as hoarding behavior, much like a fiefdom in medieval times. Of course, it didn't help to have some governing bodies appearing to be more interested in downplaying the seriousness of the virus to maintain political favor rather than relying on health science and honest messaging to a concerned and anxious public.

Most surprising, and deeply disturbing, has been the politicization of COVID-19.

On the brighter side, the speed with which the pharmaceutical industry was able to develop, test and produce effective COVID-19 vaccines is remarkable. Within a year, several vaccines deemed highly effective were approved for emergency use and made available. Other countries pursued a similar vaccination path, albeit in many cases constrained by limited vaccine availability.

On the brighter side, the speed with which the pharmaceutical industry was able to develop, test and produce effective COVID-19 vaccines is remarkable.

Yet, even with this Herculean achievement, public acceptance has been hampered by a populous who mistrust government intervention, act on misinformation, fear that there are unknown side effects, dismiss scientific evidence, or believe that getting vaccinated is an infringement on their human rights. These so-called "anti-vaxxers" represent a sufficiently large percentage of the population that their behavior inhibits the ability to achieve some form of herd immunity. This behavior has also caused resentment towards anti-vaxxers among those who have been vaccinated, asserting that the anti-vaxxers do not care about helping others.

Another dangerous outcome is that when herd immunity is not achieved in a timely manner, a virus is allowed to continue to flourish. And as a virus becomes more long-lived, chances increase that it will mutate into novel strains, creating increased risk that developed vaccines may be unable to offer protection from new versions of the disease, potentially putting us back to where we began.

There are a variety of risk mitigation actions that one can take to reduce the likelihood of contracting an infectious disease. It starts with good hygiene, washing our hands often with soap and water (or hand sanitizer when soap and water are not available). In fact, practicing good hygiene should be part of one's daily routine, not just an activity undertaken when threatened by the prevalence of an infectious disease.

The Centers for Disease Control and Prevention (CDC) provide additional guidance depending on whether the pathogen pathway is via air, food or water. When transmission is known to occur via an airborne pathway, wearing a mask that covers both our nose and mouth is important. This protects us not only from contracting the disease, but also in transmitting the disease if we are a carrier with an asymptomatic condition. To further mitigate disease transmission, it is a good habit to practice social distancing by separating from others so that any airborne pathogens are unlikely to travel that far. Further social distancing can be achieved by avoiding crowded locations and poorly ventilated indoor spaces.

Preventing disease transmission via water involves avoidance of contaminated liquids. Many of the infectious diseases associated with contaminated water are caused by pathogens transmitted by oral consumption or exposure to fecal matter. Where water treatment, sanitation and hygiene are suspect, tap water may contain disease-causing agents, making it unsafe to drink, prepare food and beverages, make ice, cook or brush teeth. Many people choose to boil, disinfect or filter their water when traveling to destinations where safe tap water may not be available.

If in doubt, it is best to rely on commercially bottled water from an unopened, factory-sealed container. An exception can be made for beverages that use water which has just been boiled, such as tea and coffee. Unopened, factory-sealed cans or bottles, carbonated beverages, commercially prepared fruit drinks, alcoholic beverages, and pasteurized drinks are generally considered safe, although the outside of cans and bottles should be wiped clean and dried before use.

Swimming in contaminated water can also be problematic. In particular, if a sore or open wound comes into contact with untreated water, it should be washed thoroughly with soap and water as soon as possible.

Contaminated food can present itself as raw or undercooked meat, fish and shellfish. In areas where hygiene and sanitation are inadequate or unknown, one should avoid consuming salads, uncooked vegetables, fruits without a peel, and unpasteurized fruit juices. In general, foods that are fully cooked and served hot are safest, particularly when self-prepared. In restaurants, inadequate refrigeration and lack of food safety preparation can result in transmission of pathogens. In particular, consumption of food and beverages obtained from street vendors should be done with caution.

We should also be mindful of underlying health conditions that can put us at increased risk of contracting an infectious disease and experiencing a more severe reaction, potentially requiring hospitalization or intensive care. Increased susceptibility of underlying health conditions will vary by the type of disease, so it is important to understand this distinction. By knowing when an underlying health condition to an infectious disease can lead to complications, the best approach to fend off this threat is disease prevention.

Actually, disease prevention is the best course of action even if we do not have an underlying condition, since there is no guarantee that one will avoid serious health consequences. What this means is if a vaccine has been tested in organized trials using strict and certifiable protocols, and it is subsequently deemed safe and effective for use by a credible public health agency, you should be encouraged to get it. Your vaccination decision should not be based on whether the vaccine is 100% effective and with no side effects, because that is not a realistic outcome. What is important is whether the vaccine is highly effective and comes with side effects that are typically temporary and not life threatening. Why? Because the downside risk of not accepting the vaccine and potentially contracting a disease that becomes a serious illness, and possibly with long-term lingering effects, far outweighs the risks associated with vaccine inoculation. In the case of COVID-19, all of the approved vaccines have produced results that show a substantial decrease in the likelihood of contracting the virus, and should by chance we get sick, a significant reduction in the likelihood of suffering serious health effects. Keeping in mind that the shield provided by these vaccines works in tandem with practicing good hygiene, as well as safe practices that uniquely apply to whether the pathogen pathway is via air, food or water, one should feel confident about the "defense in depth" that can be achieved.

Your vaccination decision should not be based on whether the vaccine is 100% effective and with no side effects, because that is not a realistic outcome.

In the event that one contracts an infectious disease, there are established protocols to help prevent disease spread to others. A best practice is to stay in isolation, quarantining at home until you are no longer contagious to others. This is not always easy, as many home environments make it difficult to find a place to quarantine for an extended period of time without coming into contact with other family members, such as sharing a bedroom, bathroom or kitchen. When this is the case, you should try to make a best effort, using good hygiene practices as a backstop.

The use of contact tracing and tracking of those who may have been exposed to someone capable of transmitting disease is another mitigation strategy that can help stop its spread. The significance of contact tracing is underscored by the realization that for each person we may have come in contact with while contagious, those people come in contact with others who become susceptible if our contacts are unknowingly contagious from spending time with us. Without contact tracing and tracking, a virus can infect a population in an exponential manner, often in rapid fashion.

A constant risk factor associated with infectious diseases has been the lack of planning and preparedness on the part of many hospitals and public health systems despite the long history of endemics, epidemics and pandemics. Much of this can be attributed to the demand on hospital facilities and medical staff to treat pandemic patients while simultaneously handling traditional medical care needs.

As many infectious diseases have the same root causes, transmission vectors, symptoms and treatments, there is no reason why public health organizations should be completely ill-prepared to address an emerging infectious disease that poses a serious threat in a rapid manner to a large population. By taking a proactive stance, one can have an off-the-shelf plan to reference should such an event occur, essentially a playbook to implement the appropriate strategic and tactical response. This could include greater reliance on telemedicine and mobile health apps to extend diagnostic capability and monitor patient conditions in real time. While this may not address every aspect of a novel disease, it puts the organization in a much better place from which to pivot than simply reacting without any prior guidance.

Additionally, the health care community has a responsibility to be part of a global surveillance network to identify a burgeoning infectious disease before it grows out of control. This requires a worldwide partnership that is grounded in truth-telling and timely notification, including sharing of the origins and characteristics of the disease. If combined with the proper messaging to potential victims, we will be better equipped to combat and overcome these disease risks and their destructive impacts.

A further consideration is the need to care about and provide for the health of the disenfranchised, vulnerable and third world populations, often dismissed altogether or considered as an afterthought. Not only is it a human rights issue, but lack of addressing this problem can also lead to a greater preponderance of infectious diseases and transmission rates that can ultimately afflict a larger population.

The most important takeaway message is that infectious diseases have been and will continue to be part of our way of life. Unfortunately, there are many reasons to believe that the emergence of future infectious diseases with the potential to become endemics, epidemics or pandemics will become more frequent. One of the unintended consequences of a global economy and the uptick in international travel is the ease with which a virus can migrate to all parts of the world that may have previously been contained and eradicated in a local area. The speed of this transmission vector makes it extremely difficult for public health organizations to identify, track and effectively curtail the spread.

The most important takeaway message is that infectious diseases have been and will continue to be part of our way of life.

Climate change is another imposing factor. There is a direct linkage between climate conditions and the propensity for infectious diseases to emerge. Diseases borne by insects with the potential to be transmitted to humans can be exacerbated with global warming and other climate-induced events on the rise. As a result, we should expect some existing health threats to intensify and new ones to emerge. In North America, for example, the population may be at increased risk in the future to contracting diseases such as Lyme, dengue fever, West Nile virus disease, and Rocky Mountain spotted fever. Moreover, infectious diseases not currently found there, such as Chikungunya, Chagas disease, and Rift Valley fever viruses, are looming threats.

> There is a direct linkage between climate conditions and the propensity for infectious diseases to emerge.

Food and waterborne diseases are also affected by climate change. Diarrheal disease is a major public health issue, most prevalent in developing countries. The transmission of pathogens in water and food that can cause diarrheal disease are known to be sensitive to air and water temperatures, precipitation patterns, extreme rainfall events, rapid snow melt and seasonal variations. For example, diarrheal diseases such as salmonellosis and campylobacteriosis are more common when temperatures are higher. These diseases also occur more frequently in conjunction with both unusually high and low levels of precipitation.

Land use is also contributing to the infectious disease conundrum. As the natural environment is cleared to support housing and economic development, it encroaches on areas where wildlife has traditionally lived and bred. This brings humans and wildlife into closer contact with one another, creating greater opportunity for infectious diseases carried by animals to be transmitted to humans. Some of the more notable pandemics have originated in this fashion.

These conditions – global travel, climate change and the land use conflict between humans and animals – are unlikely to disappear in the foreseeable future. The onus is therefore on us to be more vigilant and proactive in our approach to mitigating the risk of infectious diseases. As history has repeatedly shown, when one of these diseases rages out of control, it is difficult to contain, and the damage and suffering can be catastrophic. We should know better than to pretend that it will never happen again.

We should know better than to pretend
that it will never happen again.

Fighting Domestic Terrorism

Terrorism can be defined as the unlawful use of force or violence against persons or property to intimidate or coerce in furtherance of political, religious, social, ethnic, economic, public health or environmental objectives. Whereas international terrorism involves commission of these acts by foreign terrorist organizations or nations, domestic terrorism involves acts committed by the perpetrator's own country against fellow citizens.

Many point to September 11, 2001 as the watershed moment for international terrorism. This date in infamy coincides with the attack on the World Trade Center in New York City and the Pentagon in Washington, DC. 19 militants associated with the Islamic extremist group al Qaeda hijacked four airplanes, crashing two of them into the World Trade Center and hitting the Pentagon with a third plane. The fourth plane crashed in a field in Pennsylvania, largely due to the heroic actions of the passengers onboard who prevented the plane from reaching its desired destination.

Almost 3,000 people died from these attacks, traumatizing a nation and forever changing the war against international terrorism as we know it. This event led to a complete revamping of airline security, including hardening targets, improving intelligence gathering, actively pursuing potential perpetrators, and sanctioning nations harboring terrorist groups. These risk mitigation strategies have been largely successful in fortifying against mass casualty events committed by international terrorists on U.S. soil.

Unfortunately, despite this achievement and continued vigilance of foreign offenders, the U.S. has been unable to feel any safer from terrorist attacks, because the decline in international terrorism has been offset by a rapid increase in domestic terrorism. According to the Center for Strategic

& International Studies (CSIS), domestic terrorist attacks and plots in recent years represent the highest levels since the organization began collecting data in 1994. Much of this increase has been the result of attacks and plots orchestrated by far-right extremists.

...the decline in international terrorism has been offset by a rapid increase in domestic terrorism.

The most well-known domestic terrorist attack is arguably the Oklahoma City bombing, which took place on April 19, 1995. The assailant, Timothy McVeigh, parked a rented truck packed with an explosive comprised of agricultural fertilizer, diesel fuel and other chemicals in front of the Alfred P. Murrah Federal Building. When detonated, the bomb collapsed one-third of the building, incinerated dozens of cars and damaged or destroyed 300 nearby buildings, causing 168 fatalities and leaving several hundred injured. The motivation for McVeigh's act was attributed to his extremist ideologies and personal anger over how the federal government handled a raid two years earlier on a compound near Waco, TX to end a standoff with the Branch Davidian sect.

There are, however, other notable domestic terrorism events further back in time that have, until recently, gone relatively unnoticed. Two such events are the Wall Street Bombing and the Tulsa Race Massacre.

The bombing on Wall Street occurred on September 16, 1920. It began when an unknown assailant parked a horse drawn carriage across the street from the J.P. Morgan Building during the lunch rush and exited the vehicle. Shortly thereafter the carriage exploded, killing 30 people and injuring 300 others. Although the perpetrators were never identified, a letter carrier found four printed flyers in the area from a group of self-called anarchists that demanded the release of political prisoners. The letters appeared similar to ones discovered the previous year in two bombing campaigns instigated by Italian anarchists.

The Tulsa Race Massacre took place over an 18-hour period from May 31 to June 1, 1921, when a white mob, acting on misinformation about a supposed incident involving a black man and a white woman that was completely innocent, attacked residents, homes and businesses in the predominantly Black Greenwood neighborhood of Tulsa, OK. Most of the city's 10,000 black residents lived in this neighborhood, which included a thriving business district, referred to as Black Wall Street. In this short duration of time, 35 square blocks of the Greenwood community were turned into smoldering ashes. Countless black residents were killed — estimates range from 55 to more than 300 — and 1,000 homes and businesses were looted and set on fire. This event remains one of the worst incidents of racial violence in U.S. history.

◆ ◆ ◆

The Oklahoma City bombing ushered in an unparalleled period of domestic terrorist attacks that continues to this day. Just four years later, on April 20, 1999, two students at Columbine High School in Columbine, CO murdered twelve students and one teacher, injuring twenty-four others. And it could have been much worse, as the perpetrators also planted several homemade bombs that failed to detonate. Among the motives attributed to the attack is that these individuals had been treated as social outcasts by fellow students and were seeking revenge.

Given that the Columbine High School attack was directed at an educational facility that houses young students, many believed this event would be a catalyst for prompting major changes in the protection of school-age children. Sadly, this was not the case. More horrifying than Columbine was the attack on December 14, 2012 at Sandy Hook Elementary School in Newtown, CT. Using a semi-automatic assault rifle and two pistols, the assailant indiscriminately killed twenty-six people, including 20 children between the ages of six and seven years old. No clear motive was established other than the individual suffered from several mental illnesses.

The Sandy Hook massacre sent shock waves through the nation, as people could not conceive of anyone interested in targeting such young and innocent children. Yet, no tangible change in gun control policy occurred. Less than six years later, horror struck again, this time at the Stoneman Douglas High School in Parkland, FL on February 14, 2018. A gunman, using a semi-automatic rifle, killed 17 people and injured seventeen others. It was later discovered that the assailant had a long history of threatening behavior, yet there was no intervention.

Sadly, the number of attacks on young, innocent children and their teachers continues to grow. Just recently, high-profile attacks have taken place in Uvalde, TX and Nashville, TN. The Uvalde incident, occurring on May 24, 2022 at the Robb Elementary School, took the lives of 19 students and teachers, while injuring 17 others. On March 27, 2023, 6 students and teachers were fatally shot at the Covenant School in Nashville. In both instances, the perpetrator was a former student at the school.

Religious congregations have also been the target of domestic terrorism. On June 17, 2015, at the Emanuel African Methodist Episcopal Church in Charleston, SC, nine African Americans were killed during Bible study. The church was long known for its history and stature, including as a center for organizing civil rights events. The assailant was a young white supremacist who espoused racial hatred in a website manifesto. Three years later, on October 27, 2018, the Tree of Life Congregation in Pittsburgh, PA became a crime scene. The perpetrator, motivated by anti-Semitism, killed 11 people and injured five others. The gunman had repeatedly posted on Gab, a social media platform, that he "just wants to kill all Jews".

Disgruntled workers targeting their place of employment or former employment represents another common domestic terrorism scenario. One notable case occurred on December 2, 2015, where the Inland Regional Center in San Bernardino, CA became the site of an attack by a former employee who, along with his spouse, used automatic weapons to murder 14 health department employees and injure 22 others. Although the couple escaped from the scene, they were later killed in a shootout.

The LGBTQ+ community has also been victimized by domestic terrorists, symbolized by an attack on the Pulse nightclub in Orlando, FL on June 12, 2016. One of the city's best-known gay clubs, Pulse was filled with hundreds of party-goers when a gunman entered the club with an AR-15-type assault rifle and a handgun, forced his way inside and opened fire on the crowd. He eventually took hostages as law enforcement surrounded the building, with the standoff ending when police stormed the facility and killed the assailant. The total carnage of the event, however, numbered 49 fatalities and several injuries.

Considered by many to be the most dangerous act of domestic terrorism, threatening the ideology of democracy in the U.S. and abroad, was what has become known as the U.S. Capitol Insurrection. Occurring on January 6, 2021 at the U.S. Capitol in Washington, DC, a mob of protestors attempted to overturn President Donald Trump's defeat in the 2020 presidential election. The insurgents stormed the Capitol building and breached security while election results were being certified. The building was ransacked and five people died during the riot, including a Capitol Police officer. President Trump has been blamed for instigating the attack and, notably, criminal investigations are underway.

The events described above are by no means a complete list of domestic terrorism activities in the U.S. Rather, they are merely representative of the breadth and depth of the terrorism landscape. Moreover, the U.S. is not alone as a victim of domestic terrorism. Attacks directed at the London transit system and at a commuter rail station in Madrid, as well as the combined car bomb explosion and shootings in Norway are indicative of similar acts of domestic terrorism occurring elsewhere.

However, the U.S. stands alone when it comes to its record of domestic terrorism and not in a way that would make anyone proud. The Gun Violence Archive, a nonprofit research group that tracks gun violence using police reports, news coverage and other public sources, defines a mass shooting as an event in which at least four people are killed or injured. Using this definition, the Gun Violence Archive counted 656 mass shootings in the U.S. in 2023, making it much more than just a daily occurrence. The overwhelming conclusion is that no location in the U.S. is spared from this threat.

What makes this information so much more disturbing is that this behavior in the U.S. does not conform with what is occurring in other high-income countries and territories with populations of 10 million or more. According to the Institute for Health Metrics and Evaluation, age-adjusted firearm homicide rates in the U.S. are 13 times higher than in France, 22 times greater than in the European Union as a whole, and 23 times the rate of firearm homicides seen in Australia. When focusing on the percentage of child deaths caused by firearms, gun violence accounts for over 7% of deaths in the U.S. among those under age 20, a figure that stands far above peer countries.

There is no one-size-fits-all style of domestic terrorist attacks. They vary in motive, target, weapon, attack scenario and sophistication. As to motive, white supremacists and others who espouse white nationalist ideologies are responsible for the majority of terrorist plots and attacks in the U.S. in the past few years. In some instances, police, military and government personnel and facilities have been targeted. On other occasions, domestic terrorism has arisen from clashes between far-right and far-left groups, with violence erupting when armed individuals from opposite sides react to each other during protests and riots.

Another emerging trend is the growing number of U.S. active-duty military personnel and reservists engaged in domestic terrorist plots and attacks. In 2020, the percentage of domestic terrorist incidents linked to active-duty and reserve personnel stood at over 6%, up from less than 2% in 2019, and virtually non-existent in 2018. Similarly, a growing number of current and former law enforcement officers have been involved in domestic terrorism in recent years. Albeit a relatively small percentage of total domestic terrorism incidents as of now, this development has caught the attention of the U.S. Department of Defense (DOD), who recently issued a report to the House and Senate Armed Services Committees that concluded, "DOD is facing a threat from domestic extremists, particularly."

As the purpose of an attack is typically to cause large loss and damage and create public hysteria, targets are often locations of high-density populations or critical infrastructure. High-density populations are commonly associated with office buildings, transportation terminals, or mass gathering places like stadiums, arenas or parade routes. Critical infrastructure includes tunnels and bridges, roads on dams, drinking water supplies, information systems, utilities (e.g., gas, electricity, phone), and chemical/petroleum facilities. It can also include iconic structures like the World Trade Center, U.S. Capitol, Statue of Liberty, Golden Gate Bridge, or the Gateway Arch.

Although the attack weapon could be a firearm, vehicle, explosive, computer, fire (arson), or biological, chemical or radiological substance, the predominant weapons in domestic terrorist attacks have been firearms, vehicles and explosives, with the most frequent act involving the use of firearms. There are an overwhelming number of firearms in U.S. circulation. According to 2022 survey conducted by the University of Chicago, 46% of U.S. adults live in a household with a gun. As there are currently close to 400 million guns in circulation in the U.S., American civilians collectively own more guns than the entire population of the country. Further placing this disparity into context is that while the U.S. has just 4% of the world's population, it represents about 40% of civilian-owned guns globally. With so many guns in circulation, one can assume that virtually anybody who wants to get their hands on a gun can do so rather easily.

> As there are close to 400 million guns in circulation in the U.S., American civilians collectively own more guns than the entire population of the country.

Attack scenarios are typically characterized by the use of a specific weapon on a selected target to achieve a desired outcome. For example, if a perpetrator wanted to attack a piece of critical infrastructure, such as a water treatment plant, the following attack scenarios might be considered: 1) poisoning the water used to supply the plant, 2) exploding a bomb from a nearby vessel or vehicle, or 3) overwhelming security and entering the plant as an armed force.

It is common for attractive targets to undergo surveillance and inquiry by a perpetrator to learn more about the location and its vulnerabilities. Situational awareness can include accessibility (ability of the intruder to reach the target), hardness (effort required by the intruder to overcome the target), and interdiction (ability of security personnel to deter or intervene during an intruder attack). Additional sophistication could include performing dry runs to coordinate timing of the event and to verify prior assumptions about how the plan can be carried out.

What makes the fight against domestic terrorism so difficult is that these threats have evolved from large-group conspiracies toward lone-offender attacks, where the attacker is motivated and inspired by a mix of socio-political goals and personal grievances. These individuals often radicalize online where violent extremists have developed an extensive array of messaging platforms, online images, videos and publications, enabling a perpetrator to mobilize to violence quickly, attacking soft targets with easily accessible weapons. Without a clear group affiliation or guidance, lone offenders are challenging to identify, investigate and disrupt.

The most effective way to combat the threat of domestic terrorism is through prevention, as once an attack has been initiated, it is extremely difficult for responders to intervene before a certain amount of harm has been rendered. Prevention begins with collecting and sharing intelligence on individuals and groups whose track record or ideology are known to provoke domestic violence. This should not be solely a security agency role, as the onus is also on each of us to report suspicious behavior that we observe.

It is also important to "get in the mind" of a perpetrator by thinking through the motive, target, weapon, attack scenario and sophistication that might be employed. Recognizing that domestic terrorists are motivated by causing mass loss and damage along with hysteria, and that a perpetrator will gravitate towards targets that are highly vulnerable, it is essential to adopt a systematic and holistic approach to security risk analysis. A logical way to approach this is to implement the following steps in sequential order: 1) identify important (critical) targets, 2) define credible attack scenarios for each of these targets, 3) for each target/scenario combination, assess its vulnerability to a successful attack and the corresponding consequences, 4) create a relative risk ranking according to each target/scenario's vulnerability and consequence, 5) identify those target/scenario risks that emerge as being of high priority based on its risk ranking, 6) develop risk mitigation strategies for those high priority risks, and 7) select the most promising risk mitigation strategies for implementation.

The following hypothetical scenario illustrates how this approach can be put into action. Consider a parade for which security analysts have identified four plausible attack scenarios: 1) firearms assault, 2) ramming a truck into the crowd, 3) exploding a bomb from a nearby vehicle, and 4) releasing a deadly gas. The vulnerability of each attack scenario is assessed according to the target's accessibility, hardness and interdiction, as previously defined. The potential consequences of each attack scenario, if carried out successfully by the perpetrator(s), are evaluated taking into consideration human health, economic, social and environmental impacts.

Suppose the security analysis yields the following:

Scenario	**Vulnerability**	**Consequence**
Firearms Assault	Very High	High
Truck Ramming	High	Medium
Vehicle Bomb	Medium	Very High
Deadly Gas	Low	High

One can plot the corresponding risk of each attack scenario relative to vulnerability and consequence as follows:

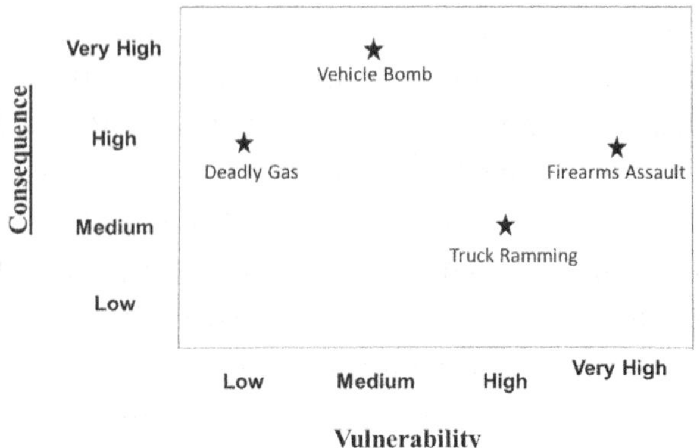

Attack Scenario Risks

The conclusion one might reach is that the firearms assault attack scenario warrants the greatest risk management attention, although not at the expense of entirely ignoring the need to address the other attack scenarios, in particular a vehicle bomb attack.

The security analyst then initiates a process of identifying candidate risk mitigation strategies for a firearms assault and evaluates their respective potential for preventing the attack, and should the attack ensue, limiting the impact. For the firearms assault attack scenario, prevention strategies might include installing security checkpoints, not allowing backpacks along the perimeter of the parade route, and increasing the number of patrol officers. Potential impact limiting strategies might include positioning snipers on building rooftops at key vantage points, placing nearby hospitals on high alert for a large influx of potential victims, and having tactical police units positioned and ready to respond. Criteria for selecting candidate strategies for deployment would rest on their respective risk reduction potential, resources required, and whether strategy implementation is practical and achievable.

Domestic terrorism is a serious and growing threat. Somewhere along the way, for whatever reason, citizens become radicalized, leading to involvement in planning and performing terrorist acts against the nation in which they reside. Because the majority of these acts are carried out by individuals, they can more easily fly under the radar, making it difficult for intelligence agencies to identify and track them until they render harm.

Despite this development, such violence should also be evaluated in broader context. The frequency and impact of domestic terrorist attacks in the U.S. is only one of many societal risks, making it important not to overstate the threat.

Still, the number of violent acts of terrorism in the U.S. is rising rapidly and this trend can be expected to continue given a current landscape characterized by political polarization, pandemics, climate change, economic stress, human migration, racial injustice, and other factors. The complexity of the threats, their intersections, and the potential for cascading events in an increasingly interconnected and mobile world presents additional challenges. Further, it is conceivable that the organizational structure of domestic terrorism could evolve from today's decentralized landscape to include more hierarchically structured groups, increasing the potency of nefarious acts.

We must also be aware of other terrorism motivators on the horizon. Of particular concern are the global food and water crises which are occurring with alarming frequency. As food and water become scarce, and people become increasingly angry and frustrated over their inability to obtain these essentials, they will also become more vulnerable to radicalization. The manner in which these developing situations are handled will largely determine the extent to which these threats spawn a new age of domestic terrorism.

Each of us can contribute to curbing domestic terrorism by serving as witnesses and responders. We need to be more observant of our surroundings, more vigilant in noticing unusual behavior, and more willing to report information through proper channels when something seems awry. Given the secrecy in how today's violent extremists conspire and act, planned attacks can be difficult for law enforcement to identify and disrupt. Often a person's family or friends may be the first to notice a concerning change in behavior that could indicate someone they know is mobilizing to violence. The worst that can happen by sharing this information is to discover that a suspicious situation was truly innocent. The worst that can happen if you don't share this information is that you have abetted a tragic outcome. The choice should be obvious.

The worst that can happen by sharing this information is to discover that a suspicious situation was truly innocent. The worst that can happen if you don't share this information is that you have abetted a tragic outcome.

Avoiding Geopolitical Conflict

Geopolitical conflict is not limited to international disputes. There are many instances of geopolitical conflict that occur within a single nation's borders, such as civil wars, arguments over water rights, or differences in ideology. Moreover, some of these controversies can be regional in nature, such as disputes between states, among states and local jurisdictions, or within local jurisdictions.

Geopolitical conflict has been intertwined with humankind going back in time as far as history has been recorded. Most of us are familiar with the Roman, Chinese and Egyptian dynasties that began thousands of years ago, mere examples of a multitude of empires that have risen and fallen over time.

Geopolitical conflict has been intertwined with humankind going back in time as far as history has been recorded.

The very nature of geopolitical conflict is a situation in which a power struggle cannot be resolved peacefully such that it becomes increasingly contentious. As tensions escalate, what initially presented itself as a threat becomes actionable, often leading to violence. This is why mitigating geopolitical risk before it reaches a violent outcome is so important. It is particularly so in light of a finding from the U.S. National Intelligence Council that no single locale is likely to dominate all regions or domains and that a broader range of actors will compete to advance their ideologies, goals and interests.

Even when a geopolitical dispute seems mostly localized in nature, the ramifications can be far-reaching. Given the interconnectedness of the world's economies and societies, a seemingly small geopolitical disturbance halfway around the globe can have a powerful impact on our quality of life if certain industries rely on products and materials that are sourced from that area. It should therefore come as no surprise that in the latest EY CEO Outlook Pulse, nearly all CEOs surveyed (97%) have altered their strategies in response to geopolitical challenges, taking actions to reconfigure their supply chains, exit businesses in certain markets, and halt a planned investment.

Of graver consequence are occurrences where a geopolitical conflict can challenge the global balance of power among democratic and autocratic ideologies. Today, these include hotspots in the South China Sea, the Middle East, and Eastern Europe. Problems of this nature can lead to large-scale human atrocities, ruin international business ventures, destroy trade agreements, or create such volatility in commodity prices that there are widespread repercussions across a variety of critical industries.

◆ ◆ ◆

The Federal Reserve has established a Geopolitical Risk Index (GPI) to assess the level of instability that exists over time due to various events. The index captures both macro events (e.g., where a country experiences a major power shift, civil war or epidemic) and risks that are considered more micro in nature (e.g., where only certain industries are affected). The GPI has been in use since the beginning of the 20th century.

As one might expect, World War I and World War II have the highest recorded GPI, given the extent and duration of the nations involved in these conflicts. The next grouping of major geopolitical conflicts includes the Gulf War, 9/11, and the Iraq invasion, followed by the Falklands War, U.S. bombing of Libya, ISIS escalation and Russia's annexation of Crimea. This latter event has blossomed into a much more significant geopolitical conflict between Russia and Ukraine. What is notable about these conflicts is that they all involved hostilities that led to significant casualties and the international community being forced to take sides, creating additional tensions that extended well beyond the initiating event itself.

It is important to note that there have been and continue to be many geopolitical conflicts whose GPI is smaller, but only in contrast to the aforementioned events. Many of these have also resulted in human carnage, displaced populations and major regime changes.

BlackRock Investment Institute publishes a geopolitical dashboard that lists the top ten most significant geopolitical risks in terms of market impact. Its most recent list is a compilation of worldwide threats that collectively show a dramatic decrease in geopolitical cooperation; or, put another way, a recipe for a very unstable political climate with potentially widespread ramifications. Among this list, the following have been identified as having a high impact likelihood:

- U.S. – China strategic competition: China's support for Russia's invasion of Ukraine, its position on potential military actions against Taiwan, and its claims in the South China Sea are potential flashpoints for significant escalation in this conflict.
- Russia – NATO standoff: Russia's large-scale invasion of Ukraine and NATO's subsequent response in terms of military support to Ukraine and extensive financial, energy and technology sanctions placed on Russia has created a hot button conflict without a diplomatic off-ramp.
- Global technology decoupling: The growing divide between China and the U.S. and its allies has driven a wedge in cooperative technological development in lieu of boosting self-reliance and reducing vulnerabilities. The semiconductor industry is a vivid example of

manufacturing independence that the U.S. and other nations are pursuing rather than enabling China to dominate the market.

- Major cyberattacks: This threat has the potential to cause sustained disruption to critical physical and digital infrastructure, effectively shutting down an opponent's ability to function or effectively retaliate. This risk has elevated as such attacks are increasing in scope, scale and sophistication.
- Gulf tensions: Although the risk of military action in this area has been a constant for decades, this threat has grown as Iran advances its mission to produce and deploy nuclear weapons, recent domestic upheaval in Israel, continued strife in Syria and Yemen, and ongoing human rights violations.

Rounding out the top ten are four other conflicts that have been rated as having medium market impact likelihood (major terror attacks, emerging markets, North Korea conflict, climate policy gridlock) and one rated as having a low market impact likelihood (European fragmentation).

Although the aforementioned geopolitical risks generally involve tensions between nations, history is replete with conflicts involving factions within the same country, sometimes resulting in civil war. The U.S. Civil War, drought and famine in many developing countries, and hostilities among warlords in the Middle East and Africa are just a few examples.

While oftentimes the impacts of civil geopolitical conflict are limited to the nation where the conflict arises, they can spill over to neighboring countries and beyond. This can take the form of other nations getting directly involved in the crises militarily or being faced with managing a large migrant population escaping the war zone. This latter situation can place considerable stress on the resources and capabilities of a receiving nation, spawning a cascading geopolitical conflict.

At a more local level, geopolitical conflict can arise between a governing region and a respective community within its jurisdiction. For example, the State of Tennessee and the City of Nashville are currently at odds over the State trying to impose control over city affairs that have traditionally been managed by the city council and local governing boards. The catalyst for this conflict stems from Nashville's decision not to pursue hosting a Republican National Convention whereas the Republican-controlled state legislature strongly desired to land the convention in Tennessee.

Finally, geopolitical conflict can be pervasive even within a local community's borders. Where to site a waste facility, prison or homeless shelter represent examples of where geopolitical conflict is almost assured.

Rarely is a single entity able to resolve a geopolitical conflict, as there are, by definition, multiple parties involved and often various other factions taking sides. While it may be possible to tone down the rhetoric or help to bide time until cooler heads can prevail, it is wise to adopt a risk mitigation strategy that is sufficiently flexible and adaptable to keep your priorities intact despite the outcome of these conflicts.

It is also helpful to treat geopolitics as a personal matter. Stakeholders who need to be directly involved in reconciling a conflict situation are likely to possess differing cultures, opinions and risk tolerances. Bringing these varying perspectives into some manner of alignment can only be possible if they can engage in candid, constructive dialogue.

Most important is to imagine all of the possible conflict scenarios and repercussions if they come to fruition in geographical areas of high strategic value. This thought process is also time-dependent, as the potential for conflict and how it proliferates can occur in days, months, years or even decades from now, with each time frame creating different types of challenges and mitigation actions. It is important in this context to have the proper expertise and to ask the right questions in order to obtain a realistic sense of the geopolitical climate.

A key strategy for keeping abreast of where geopolitics stand and how they are evolving is by developing strong relationships with organizations and individuals who are located in potential trouble spots. They have a much better understanding of what might be brewing and the likelihood of it developing into a serious threat. This level of intelligence is absolutely essential in determining if and when progressively more comprehensive risk mitigation action may be necessary. To be successful requires strong communication channels, both technological and human, that are not disrupted in case of adversity.

A key strategy for keeping abreast of where geopolitics stand and how they are evolving is be developing strong relationships with organizations and individuals who are located in potential trouble spots.

When a geopolitical threat is viewed as imminent and for which there would be significant negative impact, an organization has several risk mitigation options to consider. One possibility is to purchase insurance to cover any losses that may be incurred should the crisis reach damaging proportions. However, it can be difficult to estimate the amount of coverage that would adequately cover any loss and damage. Moreover, the insurance coverage may have specific exclusions that could negate the possibility of any payout.

Another option is to disperse critical assets such that the organization is not dependent on a single geographical site in order to maintain business continuity. This can include creating redundancy in its supply chain and distribution network such that if one part fails, normal activity can proceed. Alternatively, outsourcing to reliable vendors may be a viable option.

As mentioned earlier, under more dire circumstances, decisions can be made to exit businesses in certain markets or halt a planned investment. The departure of many businesses from operating in Russia because of its incursion of Ukraine is a notable example of the former case, whereas the latter instance is exemplified by Disney officials deciding to cancel a $1 billion development project that was previously set for Walt Disney World Resort in Florida.

Most important is maintaining a perspective and adapting accordingly. For as long as we humans inhabit the Earth, geopolitics will be inescapable, so it pays to embrace it and do our darndest to control its destructive tendencies.

Risk and Mental Health

There is no question that we are in the midst of a global mental health crisis. Here in the U.S., mental health has been deteriorating at an alarming rate.

The National Institute for Mental Health Disorders defines any mental illness (AMI) as a mental, behavioral or emotional disorder that can lead to a range in impairment from no noticeable impact to mild, moderate and even severe effects. A recent national survey conducted by the Institute estimated nearly 58 million adults aged 18 or older in the U.S. as having AMI. This number represented nearly one-quarter of all U.S. adults. The prevalence of AMI was higher among females (27%) than males (18%), with young adults (age 18-25 years) having the highest percentage of AMI. Distinctions were also noted among different races, with multiracial adults reporting the highest prevalence of AMI.

A serious mental illness (SMI) is considered a condition that results in substantial functional impairment, such that it interferes with or limits one or more major life activities. The Institute survey found an estimated 14 million adults aged 18 or older in the U.S. suffering from SMI, representing over 5% of the adult population. This reflected a similar pattern to AMI diagnoses, with a higher prevalence of SMI among females and young adults, based on gender and age, respectively. However, whereas a greater percentage of females received mental health treatment relative to their male counterparts, the opposite was true for young adults in comparison with other age groups.

Notably, many people suffer from more than one mental disorder at a particular time; for example, depressive illnesses tend to occur simultaneously with substance abuse or anxiety disorder. Anxiety disorders include panic, obsessive-compulsive behavior, post-traumatic stress disorder (PTSD), and various forms of phobia.

The connection between heightened risk perception and declining mental health can be traced to fear and anxiety that unchecked threats and overall uncertainty can have on human behavior. Typically, when we confront an extreme risk or have had a past experience that makes us feel especially vulnerable, it generates chronically higher-than-normal levels of stress. Such levels are known to suppress our immune system, disrupt normal metabolic activity, and trigger hormones that impact brain function. This can expose us to any number of mental health conditions, including depression, anxiety, substance use, sleep problems, difficulty concentrating, mood swings, and feelings of being overwhelmed and having low self-esteem. It can also increase the risk of physical health problems, such as cardiovascular disease, high blood pressure, headaches and muscle tension.

Given the current state of diminished mental health, it begs the question as to what impact emerging and growing risks, such as the ones we have discussed – climate change and extreme weather, infectious disease, social networking, cybersecurity, domestic terrorism and geopolitical conflict – have and will have on mental health. An argument can be made that the mental health risk introduced by these threats is more impactful than the the threat itself, what manifested the problem in the first place.

An argument can be made that mental health risk introduced by these threats is more impactful than the threat itself...

How serious is this connection? According to the most recent stress and current events survey conducted by the American

Psychological Association (APA), more than three-quarters of adults said that the future of our nation is a significant source of stress in their lives, while 68% felt that this is the lowest point in our nation's history that they can remember.

These stress levels often manifest themselves as symptoms with noticeable health impacts. 76% of adults participating in the APA survey reported they had experienced at least one of the following symptoms in the previous month as a result of stress: headache, fatigue, feeling nervous or anxious, and feeling depressed or sad. 72% of adults reported experiencing additional symptoms in the past month that included feeling overwhelmed, experiencing changes in sleeping habits, and worrying constantly.

In a prior APA survey, respondents judged their stress levels to be higher than what they consider to be healthy. When asked to define what constitutes a healthy stress level on a scale of 1 to 10, where a value of 1 represents little or no stress and a value of 10 is associated with a great deal of stress, on average respondents considered a value of 3.8 as a healthy level. By contrast, respondents reported experiencing, on average, a stress level of 4.9, well in excess of the healthy threshold. Younger generations reported higher stress levels than older adults.

The ensuing discussion provides additional information on the connection between mental health and the emerging and growing risks we previously introduced.

Climate change and extreme weather events can produce elevated levels of anxiety, depression and PTSD. These symptoms are often attributed to trauma and loss from human casualties, destruction of personal property, economic distress, or being disconnected from neighborhood and community.

The aftermath of these events has also been associated with increases in aggressive behavior and domestic violence.

In some cases, while terror, anger, shock and other intense negative emotions that can characterize an initial response may eventually subside, these feelings may subsequently manifest themselves as PTSD. Following Hurricane Katrina, for example, among a sample of people living in affected areas, nearly one-half developed some kind of anxiety or mood disorder, suicide and suicidal ideation more than doubled, and 1 in 6 individuals met the diagnostic criteria for PTSD.

One particular type of event, extreme heat, can be especially dangerous as it has been known to lead to increased use of alcohol to cope with stress, an uptick in hospital and emergency room admissions for people with mental health conditions, and higher instances of suicide. For people with prior mental health conditions, psychiatric medications can interfere with a person's ability to regulate heat and awareness that their body temperature is rising, increasing the likelihood of injury or death.

Besides people with mental health conditions, other population groups are particularly vulnerable to the potential impacts of climate change and extreme weather events. This includes children, emergency responders, elderly, the chronically ill, people with cognitive or mobility impairments, pregnant and postpartum women, individuals with substance use disorders, and persons who live in poverty, are migrants, refugees or homeless.

Children, for example, can be more negatively impacted by disasters than adults, due to trauma caused by disruptions in routine, separation from social networks (including as a result of evacuation or displacement), or having to endure stress exhibited by parents who are experiencing the same event themselves. Fortunately, children tend to be resilient and trauma-related symptoms may resolve over time, although long-term effects of chronic stress are certainly possible and should be closely monitored.

Climate change and extreme weather is likewise causing mental health impacts at the community level. Acute and long-term changes can elevate hostility and aggression, both interpersonal and intergroup, while also contributing to the loss of social identity and cohesion. Compounding this problem is that while the need for mental health services increases in the aftermath of a climate change or extreme weather event, there is often a disruption in services or a decrease in the availability of medical supplies at a time when they are sorely needed.

There may also be important mental health effects from potential longer-term effects of climate change. Food and water scarcity, compromised infrastructure, diminished job prospects, and other negative economic, social and environmental impacts can erode quality of life, in some cases forcing people to permanently migrate to another location. Potential increases in illnesses transmitted by insects, such as Lyme disease and malaria, and heightened air pollution that may accompany a warming climate have consequences for mental health as well, creating feelings of helplessness, fear and fatalism. If allowed to build over time, these stressors can lead to substance abuse, anxiety disorders, depression and a weakened immune system, as well as added conflict, hostility and aggression.

Regarding *infectious diseases*, as we have painfully learned from COVID-19, uncertain prognosis, shortages of resources for testing and treatment, time required to develop safe vaccines, imposition of unfamiliar public health measures that infringe on personal freedoms, financial loss, and conflicting messages are stressors that can contribute to emotional distress and increased mental health risk associated with pandemics.

In general, public health emergencies have health, safety and well-being effects on both individuals (insecurity, confusion, emotional isolation, stigma) and communities (economic loss, work and school closures, inadequate resources for medical response, deficient distribution of necessities). These effects may translate into a range of emotional reactions, including distress or psychiatric conditions, unhealthy behaviors, and noncompliance with public health directives, affecting both those who contract the disease and the general population as a whole.

Some groups appear to be more vulnerable to the psychosocial effects of pandemics. This includes individuals who contract the disease, the elderly, people with compromised immune function, those living or receiving care in congregate settings, and persons with pre-existing medical, psychiatric or substance use problems.

Health care providers are also particularly susceptible to emotional distress in pandemic settings, given their risk of exposure to the disease, concern about infecting and caring for loved ones, lack of personal protective equipment (PPE), longer work hours, and involvement in emotionally and ethically fraught resource allocation decisions. This extends to other essential workers, who are typically required to work outside of their home and may be unable to practice social distancing. Consequently, they are at increased risk of contracting the disease and exposing other household members. According to a recent Kaiser Family Foundation survey, compared to nonessential workers, essential workers were more likely to report symptoms of anxiety or depressive disorder (42% vs. 30%), starting or increasing substance use (25% vs. 11%), and having suicidal thoughts (22% vs. 8%).

Beyond stresses inherent in the illness itself, mass home confinement directives, including stay-at-home orders, quarantine and isolation, raise concern about how people will react individually and collectively. A recent review published in the New England Journal of Medicine involving a sample of quarantined people and health care providers revealed numerous emotional responses, including stress, depression, irritability, insomnia, fear, confusion, anger, frustration, boredom and stigma, some of which persisted after the quarantine was lifted. Specific stressors included greater duration of confinement, having inadequate supplies, difficulty securing medical care and medications, and resulting financial losses. In the COVID-19 pandemic, home confinement of large swaths of the population for indefinite periods, differences among stay-at-home orders issued by various jurisdictions, and conflicting messages from government and public health authorities intensified this distress.

From surveys conducted in the U.S. during the COVID-19 pandemic, as reported by the Kaiser Family Foundation, roughly 40% of adults acknowledged experiencing symptoms of anxiety or depressive disorder, a four-fold increase from the number of adults who reported these symptoms prior to the onset of COVID-19. The same poll found that many adults reported difficulty sleeping (36%) or eating (32%), increases in alcohol consumption or substance use (12%), and worsening chronic conditions (12%).

Young adults have been hit particularly hard by pandemic-related consequences, having to deal with closures of universities, transitioning to remote work, and loss of income or employment. During the pandemic, a majority of young adults (ages 18-24) reported symptoms of anxiety and/or depressive disorder. Compared to all adults, more young adults reported substance use (25% vs. 13%) and having suicidal thoughts (26% vs. 11%). In reviewing this comparison, however, one must be mindful that prior to the pandemic, young adults were already at a higher risk of poor mental health and substance use disorder.

Studies conducted during the COVID-19 pandemic also identified concerns about poor mental health and well-being for parents of young children, particularly mothers, due to challenges with school closures and lack of child care. Among women in the workplace, more than one in four considered leaving their jobs or reducing their hours, with many citing burnout and household responsibilities as the primary reason. In general, both prior to and during the pandemic, women reported higher rates of anxiety and depression when compared with men. Additionally, child abuse was purported to be more frequent during the pandemic. Child abuse can lead to immediate emotional and psychological problems and is also an adverse childhood experience linked to possible mental illness and substance misuse later in life.

The COVID-19 pandemic has also disproportionately affected the mental health of communities of color. Non-Hispanic Black adults and Hispanic or Latino adults were found to be more likely to experience symptoms of anxiety and/or depressive disorder than Non-Hispanic White adults. Compounding this problem is that communities of color have historically faced challenges with accessing mental health care. This disparate mental health impact comes in addition to Black and Hispanic communities experiencing disproportionately high rates of coronavirus cases and deaths, and negative financial impacts. Black parents more often than White parents also reported negative impacts of the pandemic on their children's education, ability to care for their children, and relationships with family members.

As one might expect, adults in poor physical and/or mental health prior to the pandemic continued to report higher rates of anxiety and/or depression than other adults. For people suffering from a chronic illness, the already high likelihood of having a concurrent mental health disorder appears to have been exacerbated by their vulnerability to severe illness from COVID-19. With older adults being more vulnerable to severe illness from coronavirus, they too have experienced increased levels of anxiety and depression during the pandemic.

Among adults reporting symptoms of anxiety and/or depressive disorder, more than 20% reported needing, but not receiving, counseling or therapy in the prior month during the COVID-19 pandemic. Such limited access to mental health care and substance use treatment can be attributed in part to a shortage of mental health professionals, which is exacerbated during a pandemic. The pre-pandemic shortage of psychiatric hospital beds also worsened with the surge of COVID-19 patients needing this level of care.

Access to mental health and substance use care was already a big concern prior to the pandemic. In 2018, among the 6.5 million non-elderly adults experiencing serious psychological distress, only 44% reported seeing a mental health professional in the past year. Compared to adults without serious psychological distress, adults with serious psychological distress were more likely to be uninsured (20% vs. 13%) and unable to afford mental health care or counseling (21% vs. 3%). For people with insurance coverage, an increasingly common barrier to accessing mental health care was a lack of in-network options for treatment.

History has shown that the mental health impact of disasters outlasts the physical impact, suggesting today's elevated mental health need will likely continue well beyond the COVID-19 outbreak itself. For example, a recent assessment of the toll on health care providers during disease outbreaks found that psychological distress can last up to three years after an outbreak.

History has shown that the mental health impact of disasters outlasts the physical impact...

Heavy use of and increasing reliance on *social networking* can put many of us at increased risk of feeling anxious, depressed, lonely, envious, and even ill. Excessive social media use can also lead to self-absorption, impulse control issues and lack of concentration, jeopardizing work or school performance, as well as personal and business relationships. Moreover, this obsession can limit time for self-care activities such as mindfulness, self-reflection and exercise, thereby reinforcing the problem.

One notable mental health phenomenon associated with social media is the fear of missing out. We humans are social beings who desire group interaction, and perceived exclusion can have damaging psychological impacts, including anxiety and depression. To avoid missing out, however, excessive use of social media can produce an unhealthy way of coping with uncomfortable feelings or emotions, rather than addressing them in a constructive manner.

Compulsive use is also dangerous, especially if gratification is not received, as we may believe it is due to being unpopular, not funny, or some other negative connotation. Moreover, a lack of "likes" on a status update may prompt a need to continually refresh the page, hoping that someone will respond favorably, thus helping to achieve personal validation. Worst yet, it might prompt engagement in risky behaviors such as posting outrageous photos in order to gain approval. Ultimately, the lack of positive feedback online, especially if it involves being trolled or cyberbullied by others, can lead to self-doubt and self-hatred.

Additionally, social media can cause us to experience feelings of inadequacy about our lives and our appearance. Images posted online that have been manipulated or represent someone's highlight reel can promote unreasonable expectations if we compare ourselves with these appearances, causing feelings of insecurity, poor self-esteem and self-image, envy and dissatisfaction. In particular, the notion of an ideal body image can be detrimental, especially for young women.

Also associated with the desire for gratification is the negative impact that social media can have on sleep and sleep quality. Sleep loss works in a vicious cycle of reinforcement with mental health, where lack of sleep leads to poorer mental health, which subsequently leads to additional sleep loss.

Young people are particularly vulnerable. As reported in Psychology Today, studies have found that young people who use social media more than two hours per day are more likely to categorize their mental health as fair or poor when compared to occasional social media users. Moreover, heavy users of social media are three times more likely to experience symptoms of depression than occasional users.

Some mental health professionals argue that the psychological effects of *cybersecurity* breaches may even rival those of traditional terrorism, with data breaches and other cybercrimes taking a heavier psychological toll on the millions of people whose personal information has been compromised for nefarious means. Moreover, cyberattacks are becoming more technically complex and damaging, further impacting our feelings, emotions and behaviors.

Much of the mental impact is induced by the nightmarish process of clearing our name and credit history, or the struggle to get credit or loans, housing, employment or medical services after a breach. Victims wrestle with feelings of powerlessness and vulnerability, which often leads to disruptive sleep, decreased energy levels, and greater involvement in drug and alcohol use. For some, the aftereffects are more severe, including bouts of depression and anxiety, even PTSD. In more extreme cases, the ramifications of data theft can lead to job loss, divorce and suicide. Making the problem more complex is that with every breach, it serves as a reminder of these feelings, leading to the possibility of becoming retraumatized.

According to a survey of identity theft victims conducted by the Identity Theft Resource Center, 86% of respondents reported feeling worried, angry and frustrated. Nearly 70% said they could not trust others and felt unsafe. More than two-thirds reported feelings of powerlessness or helplessness, while sadness or depression afflicted 59%. One-half of the victims reported losing interest in activities or hobbies they once enjoyed.

These negative emotions also had physical repercussions. Nearly 85% reported disturbances in sleep habits, 77% noted increased stress levels and roughly 64% said they had trouble concentrating. Aches, pains, headaches and cramps were symptoms for nearly 57% of respondents.

Consumers are not the only ones at mental health risk associated with cybersecurity. On the front lines of a high-stress occupation, cybersecurity professionals shoulder the heavy responsibility of protecting our data. These folks frequently describe being in a constant state of high alert, even when not on the job. When a breach does occur in an area of their responsibility, guilt and shame are common reactions. Moreover, for these employees, the threat of the stolen data being exploited is sometimes just as traumatic as the reality of it happening.

Due to the nature of this profession, depression, burnout and suicide are becoming more common among cybersecurity professionals. While workplace stress is not unique to this industry, pressure is intense in trying to stay abreast with cybercriminals who are constantly devising new methods of penetrating systems, making it challenging to keep up in a never-ending battle.

Because of this at-risk environment and the proliferation of cyberattacks, it should come as no surprise that a labor shortage exists in this industry, placing even greater stress on workers who are asked to bear even larger roles and responsibilities. A recent survey of Chief Information Security Officers (CISOs) conducted by Cynet found that 94% of them are stressed at work. In addition, 65% of survey respondents admitted that work-related stress is compromising their ability to protect their organization.

The survey also revealed that cybersecurity team members are leaving their positions at a significant rate, with 74% of cybersecurity leaders reporting that they are losing team members due to work-related stress issues. This high turnover rate is also affecting recruitment efforts.

One other interesting aspect involves the fact that the cybersecurity field attracts many ex-military members, some who have existing PTSD from their previous deployments. This pre-existing condition may be a contributing factor to the increasing rate of mental health issues in the cyber workspace.

Unaddressed mental health issues can also have serious ramifications when it comes to the actual practice of cybersecurity. Since cybersecurity professionals and criminal hackers each have the ability to manipulate their target, what separates the good from the bad may be their mental health. Sufficient employee stress, depression or anxiety can lead to erratic urges that may manifest itself in stealing data or destroying the very systems these professionals have been asked to protect.

Terrorism of any kind, and *domestic terrorism* in particular, is intended to provoke collective fear and uncertainty. These feelings can spread rapidly and are not limited to those experiencing the event directly. Others who may be affected include family members of victims and survivors, emergency responders, and people who are exposed through various media. Commonly reported effects include PTSD, major depression, and general psychological distress.

Terrorist attacks, and the threat of a terrorism event, may also result in more severe psychological consequences than other types of traumatic events due to a perceived lack of control. In these circumstances, it becomes less effective to cope by distancing oneself from the population at risk if the risk is seemingly random. For example, the degree of public anxiety resulting from the 2001 Washington, D.C. area random sniper attacks was considered much greater than the anxiety levels related to the violence that is endemic to many Washington, D.C. areas.

Beyond impacts felt by affected individuals, terrorism has the capacity to erode the sense of community or national security, damage morale and social connectedness, and exacerbate racial, ethnic, economic and religious rifts that exist in our society. This often leads to expanded threats to community cohesion and to the psychological well-being of those who are the targets of discrimination.

In the case of the 1995 Oklahoma City bombing, PTSD was reported by approximately one-third of survivors of the direct bomb blast six months after the bombing, and nearly three-fourths of them were individuals with no prior history of PTSD. Increases in school or work absenteeism have also been observed following terrorist attacks. Additionally, terrorism-related mental health impacts can include increased school dropout, divorce, and domestic or interpersonal conflict and violence.

Others experiencing mental health symptoms can include persons in close geographic proximity to the incident, exposed to the event through the media, negatively impacted through secondary effects such as an economic downturn, and who experience the death of or immediate risk to a victim of the event itself (e.g., relatives, friends, co-workers, rescue workers, witnesses). Additionally, a person's prior experience of a traumatic event may be related to psychological consequences following a terrorism event.

Gender, age, and experience have all been connected to magnified adverse outcomes. Females suffered worse short-term impacts in the aftermath of September 11, 2001 according to a number of studies of the general population. The psychological impact of terrorist attacks on children and adolescents is also frequently noted.

Disaster mental health literature is replete with findings that first responders and rescue workers are at risk for adverse psychological outcomes after responding to a disaster, likely due to their direct and often ongoing exposure to traumatic experiences. On November 13, 2015, terrorist attacks took place at six different locations in and around Paris, killing 129 people with over 300 others requiring emergency care. As reported in the Journal of Psychiatric Research, nearly one-third of health professionals from Parisian hospitals who attended to the victims were judged to be at high risk for some combination of PTSD, anxiety and depression, roughly twice the level reported by non-exposed health professionals. The most significant mental health symptoms were associated with those who witnessed the attacks or had a close relative among the victims, but they were also reported by first responders who cared for patients at the sites of the massacre. Women were observed to be at higher risk of developing PTSD than men, a result consistent with other studies, which also concluded that PTSD persists longer in women, particularly after exposure to interpersonal trauma. Furthermore, the incidence of PTSD has been reportedly higher for survivors of terrorist attacks than for survivors of other traumatic situations such as motor vehicle accidents or natural disasters.

While it is clear that some populations may be particularly vulnerable to adverse outcomes following a terrorism event, the duration and intensity of exposure to the event can be a discerning factor. Although many people exhibit some manifestation of distress in the aftermath of a terrorism event, certain symptoms have been identified as being more predictive of later psychiatric illness. These include feeling numb, becoming withdrawn or disconnected, isolating from others, and avoiding activities, places or people that bring back memories of the event.

Yet, terrorism events, like other disaster events, can also produce unique positive outcomes for a community. Because terrorism is generally directed at a population or sub-population, there is often a growth in patriotism and pride following the event. For example, after the terrorism events on September 11, 2001, many people reported an increased appreciation for the freedom afforded by living in the U.S. They also reported closer relationships with family members subsequent to those attacks.

The National Library of Medicine acknowledges that health can be shaped by *geopolitical conflict*, including war, famine, colonization, and oppression of minorities. As reported in PLOS One, the mechanism by which politics can harm health is fairly well understood. Politics are a chronic stressor, saturating popular culture and permeating daily life through social media, various entertainment platforms and a 24-hour news cycle. Politics influence social networks and individual identity, and is a well-documented source of negative emotions that can decrease psychological and physical well-being.

According to a Queens University study nearly 40 percent of Americans felt that politics was a source of significant anxiety, insomnia and even suicidal thoughts. The APA also identified politics as a major source of stress for adults, associating increased rates of depression, anxiety, loss of sleep, and emotional reactivity among groups, particularly among people with high levels of opposition to the government in power at the time.

Political elections and the events leading up to them have been recognized as a significant source of stress. Moreover, supporters of losing candidates engage in more stress-related behaviors such as increased alcohol consumption, and greater exposure to political campaign ads also increases the likelihood of suffering from fatigue, sleep deprivation, anxiety or depression.

In addition to the aforementioned impacts, politically-induced stress has been associated with physiological impairment. Political engagement has been found to correlate with baseline levels of cortisol, with witnessing political conflict increasing activation of the nervous system. This can lead to feelings of anger and loss of temper, as well as triggering compulsive behaviors (e.g., obsession with thinking about politics and consuming political information), and difficulties in impulse control (e.g., posting social media comments they later regret).

The disturbing news is that the so-called *risk elephants in the room* – climate change and extreme weather, infectious disease, social networking, cybersecurity, domestic terrorism, and geopolitical conflict – are producing new stressors that are exacerbating and continuing to erode and polarize an already fragile society. The good news, however, is that there is great commonality in how these stressors manifest themselves in terms of mental health effects.

> The good news, however, is that there is great commonality in how these stressors manifest themselves in terms of mental health effects.

This suggests that it is not the unique characteristics of each of these evolving risks that require risk management attention, but rather the devolving process by which these risks influence our perceptions, emotions, mental capacities and behaviors. If we can construct and practice a healthy means of recognizing and acting on the triggers associated with this process, we can manage these and other risks more effectively. By doing so, it may even be possible to turn some of these risks into opportunities by being proactive rather than reactive.

> ...it may even be possible to turn some of these risks into opportunities by being proactive rather than reactive.

It is important, however, to acknowledge that the inability to manage risk is not entirely responsible for the occurrence of mental illness or the preponderance of people afflicted with this condition. The psychology behind the human response to stress and how it manifests itself in individual behavior is far more complex than simply inferring a one-to-one relationship between heightened risk perception and poor mental health. However, it is undeniable that there is a clear connection in this association. Any time that a person is experiencing chronic stress attributed to risks that are impacting their life, a pattern emerges that can lead to this potential end point. It therefore stands to reason that improving our risk management practices reduces this possibility.

A key to combating the potential negative psychological effects of ongoing or emerging risks is by building psychological resilience through self-care. As it is important that we find a channel to voice what is happening to us, such as feelings of grief, guilt, anger or rage, surrounding ourselves with a social network that is supportive and that we can trust is a healthy practice.

A key to combating the potential negative psychological effects of ongoing or emerging risks is by building psychological resilience through self-care.

Changing the pattern of negative thinking is another strategy in the mental health toolbox, as this thought process can lead to a downward spiral. Instead, try to imagine positive scenarios, and identify a role that enables you to achieve that outcome.

Maintaining a positive outlook often revolves around how to handle uncertainty. Accepting that there will be uncertainty in most of what we encounter can free us to focus on what is in our control. It has been suggested that trying something new, traveling somewhere unfamiliar, or going without a schedule can help one become more comfortable with the unknown and our ability to handle it.

Adopting environmentally friendly policies and lifestyle choices can also have a positive effect on mental health. Increased accessibility to parks and other green spaces can be beneficial, as spending more time in nature has been known to lower stress levels and reduce stress-related illness, regardless of socioeconomic status, age or gender. Maintaining an active level of physical exercise is also known to improve mental health; hence, the adage *strong in body, strong in mind.*

At times it can make sense to take your own advice. For example, if a friend comes to you with a similar worry, what would you tell them? Imagining your situation from the outside can often provide perspective and fresh ideas.

Prevention efforts such as screening for mental health problems, along with psychological education and social support, should focus on individuals at risk for adverse mental health outcomes. However, opportunities to monitor these needs and deliver support are greatly curtailed when crises such as pandemics lead to large-scale home confinement. Fortunately, psychosocial services, normally delivered in primary care settings, are increasingly being offered by means of telemedicine. In the context of COVID-19, psychosocial assessment and monitoring can include queries about pandemic-related stressors (e.g., exposure to infected sources, infected family members, loss of loved ones, and physical distancing), secondary adversities (e.g., economic loss), psychosocial effects (e.g., depression, anxiety, psychosomatic preoccupations, insomnia, increased substance use, and domestic violence), and indicators of vulnerability (e.g., preexisting physical or psychological conditions). Some patients will need referral for formal mental health evaluation and care, while others may benefit from supportive interventions designed to promote wellness and enhance coping. For example, suicidal ideation may emerge and necessitate immediate consultation with a mental health professional or referral for possible emergency psychiatric hospitalization.

On the milder end of the psychosocial spectrum, many experiences of affected persons can be successfully addressed by providing information about usual reactions to different kinds of stress and by pointing out that people can and do manage even in the midst of seemingly dire circumstances. Health care providers can offer suggestions for stress management and coping (such as structuring activities and maintaining routines), link patients to social and mental health services, and counsel patients to seek professional mental health assistance when needed. Since media reports can be emotionally disturbing, contact with some news sources should be monitored and limited. Because parents commonly underestimate their children's distress, open discussions should be encouraged to address their reactions and concerns.

As for health care providers themselves, when disaster strikes and particularly if the impacts persist, inadequate testing, limited treatment options, insufficient medical supplies, and extended workloads are sources of stress with the potential to overwhelm systems. Moreover, similar to cybersecurity professionals, burnout can easily lead to flight from the profession, leaving resources even more strained. Self-care for mental health care providers involves being informed about the risks, monitoring personal stress reactions, and seeking professional mental health intervention if indicated. Health care systems will need to address the stress on individual providers and on general operations by monitoring reactions and performance, altering assignments and schedules, modifying expectations, and creating mechanisms to offer psychosocial support, including education and training, when needed.

And there is reason to be optimistic. Despite the myriad of stressors to deal with, as reported by the American Psychological Association, a recent survey found that over 70% of adults reported that they feel hopeful about their future, with an equal number saying that they can get things done even when feeling stressed.

Part III - Staying on the Wall

We've covered the basics of risk perception, communicating risk, and what we should be worrying about. We also discussed risks that are looming and growing, including the implications on mental health. Now it's time to put this all together into a structured approach to successfully managing your risk portfolio, otherwise known according to Humpty Dumpty as *staying on the wall.*

There are several aspects to making the wall a safe and secure place. It begins by understanding the risk factors that threaten to undermine our stability. Those factors form the basis of a multitude of risk scenarios that we should consider, ones that are likely to be so diverse in our modern world that it requires an enterprise risk management approach. In adopting this perspective, one can benefit immensely by reviewing important lessons learned from past history. To bring the enterprise risk management approach into a practical and easy-to-use process, risk dashboard tools and rules of engagement are introduced that one can apply on a personal or professional level.

Staying on the wall is not likely to happen by luck or good fortune. It requires a concerted and directed effort at establishing and maintaining best risk management practices.

Key Risk Factors

Why do bad things happen? With all of our knowledge, skill and technology, can't we do something to prevent them or at least keep them from causing such harm?

Misfortunes come in many forms, which can be conveniently organized into three groups. *Man-made accidents* are the result of human action or inaction that starts a chain of events leading to an unfortunate outcome. These errors in judgment, however, may not be intentional or malicious. By contrast, *terrorist acts* are conscious decisions made by individuals and groups with purposeful and destructive intent. These acts are typically well-planned, with a specific target in mind, often directed at causing heavy casualties and creating mass hysteria. The final category, *natural disasters*, are considered acts of God, with most natural disasters attributed to extreme weather events or movement of the earth's crust. Although it is debatable as to whether humans are responsible for the occurrence of some natural disasters, it is clear that our actions can have a profound impact on the severity of the consequences when such events occur.

While these groups of undesirable events may seem rather different in their appearance, when taking a closer look at how they evolve, there is remarkable similarity. In other words, there emerges a pattern or "recipe" for disaster. What are the ingredients to this recipe and how do they interact to form such a lethal outcome? Below are listed underlying risk factors that when present, alone or in combination with other risk factors, can erode our margin of safety to a point where a situation is free to unravel to potentially epic proportions.

...risk factors that, when present, alone or in combination with other risk factors, can erode our margin of safety to a point where a situation is free to unravel to potentially epic proportions.

Design or Construction Flaws

When facilities or products are constructed, they are normally built according to detailed design specifications. These specifications should be based on engineering analyses that ensure the structural design can withstand the demands that will be imposed upon it, such as load, vibration and power, among other considerations. If there is a flaw in the design process that jeopardizes whether these demands can be met, it can become prone to failure, potentially leading to a serious outcome.

However, even if the design is valid, problems can still arise if the materials used to fabricate the components are faulty or the components are not assembled properly. In either case, the integrity of the product is compromised, making it susceptible to failure, with similar outcomes to when a design flaw is present.

A classic case involving this risk factor involved the construction of the Hyatt Regency hotel in Kansas City. A dance hosted in the hotel atrium in October 1981 ended in tragedy when the second and fourth-floor skywalks collapsed onto a crowded dance floor, leaving 114 people dead and another 216 injured. Flaws in a simple design change made to a support mechanism went unnoticed, allowing the skywalk to buckle at the worst possible moment.

Deferred Maintenance

In the helter-skelter of trying to keep an operation up and running, if a problem is discovered that requires maintenance, it spurs a debate of whether to shut down the operation and fix the problem immediately, or to keep going and defer the repair to a more convenient time. This decision involves weighing the risk of deferring maintenance against the benefit of maintaining continuous operations. In such instances, it is human nature to opt to deal with problems at a later time, especially if the system is not actually malfunctioning. Unfortunately, decisions to defer maintenance, both in personal matters and for organizations, often lead to the failure of a key system component before the repair can be made, causing an accident to occur. Deferred maintenance on our aging transportation infrastructure is a well-known problem, and one that has safety analysts concerned given the overuse of our roads and bridges relative to the expected demand for which these facilities were originally designed.

Within a culture where maintenance problems are customarily deferred, the situation also becomes ripe for multiple component failures, allowing the consequences of the ensuing accident to propagate and intensify. A well-known example of this behavior involves what is arguably the most catastrophic event to ever hit the chemical industry – Bhopal, India. In December 1984, a combination of clogged drainage, leaky valves, uncalibrated temperature and pressure gauges, and non-functioning refrigeration and alarm systems created a nightmare scenario that led to a massive release of methyl isocyanate, a highly toxic material that is extremely hazardous to human health. This caused thousands of fatalities and injuries, as well as serious long-term health effects for many others.

Schedule or Financial Constraints

As one might expect, two of the more common risk factors involve time and money. When against a deadline and tasks have fallen behind schedule, pressure to make up ground can cause us to cast a blind eye towards important details. This can lead to the elimination of critical tasks, trying to accomplish tasks in parallel that should be done in sequence, or not pursuing certain considerations in sufficient depth to fully understand their impact. Such conduct creates an environment that is ripe for committing errors in judgment that result in an unfortunate outcome.

Virtually anything we undertake is constrained by limited financial resources. When a budget is too tight or spending is not adequately controlled, pressure intensifies to implement cost-cutting measures. This can translate into shoddy workmanship, purchasing lower quality materials, eliminating the use of safety equipment, or ignoring problems that arise.

Although it is possible that either schedule or financial constraints can act alone to produce a high-risk environment, they often work together to create an unwanted outcome. It is not unusual for a project to be simultaneously running over budget and behind schedule, a popular breeding ground for critical mistakes and poor decision-making.

In March 1989, the crew of the *Exxon Valdez* grounded the vessel on a reef located in Alaska's Prince William Sound, puncturing the cargo hold and allowing 11 million gallons of crude oil to escape, contaminating one of the world's most pristine areas. A key risk factor contributing to this event involved a shortage of crew members aboard the vessel, a reduction in force that was made for economic reasons. As a result, crew members were often overworked, regularly putting in 12 to 14-hour days. It has been estimated that at the time of the accident, the officer on the bridge (and in charge of vessel navigation) had been working for 18 consecutive hours, potentially impairing his judgement and fitness to command the ship.

Ignoring the Plight of Socially Vulnerable Populations

Our society is composed of many different sub-populations, often defined by demographic characteristics. Many of these groups are underprivileged or subject to discrimination, placing them in a vulnerable position for experiencing and responding to risky situations. Income, employment status, religion, race, ethnicity, sexual orientation and political beliefs all represent demographic characteristics that can potentially serve as factors which exacerbate risk.

Often, heightened risk scenarios are imposed on socially vulnerable populations in crisis situations. It is well-documented how a socially vulnerable population in New Orleans was mistreated during and in the aftermath of Hurricane Katrina. More than one-quarter of the people living in New Orleans when Hurricane Katrina struck lived below the poverty line, and much of this population had no choice but to remain at home to weather the storm, suffering greatly as a result. This was due to a combination of social vulnerability factors, including lack of car ownership, inadequate communication technology, and absence of economic means to afford lodging elsewhere. The one hope, emergency evacuation by bus, failed because the city had parked its buses in a location that flooded, rendering these vehicles inoperable at a time of utmost need.

Communication Failure

This risk factor is present in nearly every disaster scenario, contributing to the cause, the impact, or both. Communication failures can occur at various stages, altering an outcome in different ways. One common form of communication failure can occur between members of the same team. In this instance, critical information is not shared, such as when one group decides to shut down a protection system for maintenance while another group is carrying out a dangerous experiment. Or in the case of a personal situation, when family members withhold sensitive information so as not to embarrass themselves.

Poor communication between parties is also problematic; for example, when two agencies engaged in a response effort are unaware of what the other is doing. Finally, lack of communication with the public or the dissemination of inaccurate information can place us at risk either by not knowing the hazards we are facing, or by not being properly advised of how to protect ourselves.

History is replete with examples of how failed communication contributed to tragic outcomes, including the deadliest accident in aviation history, claiming 583 victims. This catastrophic event occurred in March 1977, when two Boeing 747 passenger jets, one belonging to the KLM fleet and the other to Pan Am, collided on the runway at an airport on the island of Tenerife. With fog causing reduced visibility for the pilots and the control tower, the KLM pilot relied on radio communication for clearance to takeoff. Mistakenly believing that such clearance had been received, the pilot sped down the runway and collided with the Pan Am aircraft that stood in its path.

Lack of Planning and Preparedness

Planning and preparedness are proactive efforts focused on expending resources in advance of a threat to improve understanding and be in a position to implement risk mitigation initiatives before a problem arises. Depending on the nature of the threat, attention can be directed at preventing an undesirable event from occurring, limiting the impact of an event once it has occurred, or both. Planning and preparedness activities can include gathering knowledge, assessing the likelihood and consequence of various scenarios, evaluating and implementing risk reduction strategies, conducting exercises to determine the effectiveness of ongoing efforts, and maintaining a state of readiness.

Unfortunately, because of other seemingly more immediate priorities or that a particular disaster scenario may not have been experienced in recent memory, we tend to place a lower priority in terms of the effort and resources required to adequately prepare for a crisis situation. This can create circumstances where little forethought is given to disaster scenarios that might occur, the magnitude and impact of these events are underestimated if the scenario is considered, or the ability to adequately handle a crisis situation is overestimated. Even where significant effort is devoted to planning and preparedness, the product of this effort could be a document that is not practiced or updated, rendering it of little value when a calamity arises.

The extent of the COVID-19 pandemic can arguably be traced to a lack of planning and preparedness. In the U.S., federal government authorities showed little interest in preparing for the possibility of a pandemic, such that insufficient attention was devoted to how the problem could arise and how to respond. Although the prospect of a pandemic crippling the nation had been discussed, nobody anticipated that COVID-19 could spread so rapidly and render such devastating health effects. Moreover, it was generally assumed that the health care community would have adequate capability to combat the disease if it proliferated.

Consequently, when COVID-19 arrived and infection rates intensified, precious time was lost in trying to devise a strategy for combatting the virus while it exercised its wrath. By the time the spread of the disease had reached alarming proportions, only then did a response emerge, one that was plagued by a lack of resources, logistical nightmares, poor communication and failed leadership. Adding to the misery was knowledge that the previous federal government administration had taken the possibility of a pandemic seriously and had developed a playbook of strategies to manage such a crisis, yet the succeeding administration chose to ignore its existence. This lack of planning and preparedness created a confusing, conflicting and generally incomprehensible response effort. We are left to ponder how many hundreds of thousands of lives may have been saved, businesses survived, and communities left intact had planning and preparedness been taken more seriously.

Inadequate Legal/Regulatory Standards or Compliance

Laws and regulations are typically enacted to protect individuals and businesses from situations that can threaten their well-being. Oftentimes, these laws and regulations do not adequately cover the breadth and depth of what might arise. This can create loopholes that lead to an unfortunate event or significantly impair the ability to respond and recover. In some cases, these loopholes are actually exploited with purposeful intent. It is not uncommon, for example, for certain high-hazard industries, such as oil & gas, chemical manufacturing and mining, to circumvent environmental laws by claiming to be exempt from having to comply, putting populations and species at greater risk.

In other instances, laws and regulations have been established to mitigate a specific risk, but are not adequately enforced or blatantly ignored. Governments attempting to become more economically competitive, for example, are often willing to relax safety standards in order to attract business. A well-known example is the case in many Asian countries involving the garment manufacturing industry. Numerous incidents have occurred where lax safety practices were employed, yet little was done to address the problem for fear that these industries would merely move to a competitor nation. The April 2013 collapse of the Rana Plaza garment factory building in Dhaka, Bangladesh, which killed over a thousand people and injured many others, serves as a vivid reminder of this unfortunate practice. The building was originally planned for shops and offices rather than for factory use; moreover, several floors were constructed without a permit. As the resulting structure was not capable of bearing the weight and vibration of heavy factory machinery, it was only a matter of time before the building would give way.

Equally nefarious is when a sweetheart deal has been arranged between the regulating agency and a company subjected to that regulation such that the company is given a pass. This often occurs when the compliance officer used to work for the industry sector, prior to joining the regulating agency, or vice-versa. The mining industry has been cited on many occasions as a bad actor in this regard.

Lack of Training or Experience

Many of today's tasks have become more complicated by the complexity of technological innovation and the highly integrated nature of various systems. Consequently, the performance of many important functions requires us to be well-trained. However, some organizations view training as a burden that is costly to perform, as the employee is not generating revenue while being trained. This short-sighted perspective can place one in a position of responsibility where their lack of training causes a mistake to be made that either initiates an accident or allows a crisis situation to intensify.

One industry where this risk factor has been prominent involves drivers of heavy commercial trucks. These vehicles can carry up to 80,000 pounds gross vehicle weight, oftentimes hurtling down a highway at speeds in excess of 60 mph. Most of us have witnessed a heavy truck accident, in many instances involving passenger vehicles as well. More often than not, it is the occupants of the passenger vehicle who suffer the greatest harm, due to the tremendous differential in momentum (mass times velocity) between these vehicle types when they collide. Because there is a severe shortage of truck drivers to meet truck transportation demand, it is widely speculated that truck drivers are being hired to satisfy this need who are not sufficiently qualified to operate a heavy and dangerous rig due to inadequate training and experience.

Problems with inadequate training can go beyond when someone first gets involved in an activity. When there are personnel shortages, an employee may be thrown into a role and responsibility while covering for someone else, performing a function for which they may not be properly trained. Even if previously trained, one can be susceptible to forgetting what they were originally taught or processes have changed over time that require new learning, making lack of re-training also an emergent risk factor.

Complacency

When engaged in a repetitive activity, complacency can set in, and we tend to drift away from following a strict protocol. Hence, we either neglect to perform certain steps or invent other ways to accomplish the same task, often not considering the safety ramifications of our actions. Not only can complacency create a hazardous situation, but it can also be exacerbated by others whose actions are based on assuming that we have successfully performed our role and responsibility.

Most organizations have well-defined procedures for how an employee should perform a task or function. These are often documented and made available during training and as a reference when on the job. Moreover, job supervisors have a duty to ensure that each direct report is following standard procedures. Surprisingly, this is one of the most vulnerable places for the root cause of a failure to occur.

Construction workers are notorious for exhibiting complacency while on the job. In 2019, construction-related deaths represented one-fifth of all workplace fatalities in the U.S. Many safety regulations have been instituted to protect construction workers from having debilitating accidents, yet it is common for them to get hit by falling debris while milling around a site, slipping or falling on a roof or above the ground floor on a multi-story building and not wearing a safety harness, getting trapped between materials, or touching a live wire. Many of these events can be attributed to complacency, a common malady among construction workers who lose sight of their risk having performed repetitive functions on a continual basis without incident.

Arrogance or Greed

These risk factors are human traits that can complicate what might otherwise be a low-risk proposition. Arrogance or greed can rear its head in many forms, but usually appears as a person or entity driven to succeed for individual gain without regard for the well-being of others. This can create an environment of concerns being expressed by others that fall on deaf ears or, worse yet, a culture of fear of reprisal that prevents problems from being divulged in the first place.

Another common scenario occurs when an individual or organization has become overconfident in their ability to solve a glaring problem. The result is a tendency to underestimate the risk at hand or fail to act in a purposeful fashion, believing that, "I've seen everything before and was able to handle it", or "This is not going to get the better of me."

Such was the case with the final voyage of the *Edmund Fitzgerald*. In November, 1975, this commercial vessel sank in Lake Superior during a freak early-winter storm. Of the 29 crew members aboard, nobody was ever found, motivating Gordon Lightfoot to memorialize the tragedy in a famous song. Among the risk factors cited as contributing to the *Fitzgerald's* demise were a greedy company economic policy to maximize cargo movement and arrogance exhibited by the ship's captain driven by his pride as a seasoned sailor who believed he could overcome whatever weather Mother Nature might throw at him. In hindsight, the ship should not have set sail so late in the season, and when the winter storm began and subsequently strengthened, the captain should have sheltered in a safe harbor, as other similar vessels did, rather than trying to ride out the storm surge.

Lack of Oversight

When things go wrong, it is often the result of decisions and actions taken without the counsel and supervision of an oversight body. As a result, situations are allowed to run amuck when, in retrospect, if the oversight body had been more closely involved, the disaster could have been averted. In most organizations, the oversight role rests with senior management or an executive board, while oversight in personal matters often falls on a family member or respected advisor.

The need for adequate oversight cannot be overemphasized. The National Aeronautics and Space Administration (NASA) is a poster child when it comes to oversight gaffes and the catastrophic outcomes it can produce. For both the Challenger and Columbia space shuttle disasters, in which the entire flight crew perished, post-accident investigations found compelling evidence of NASA institutional failures as a root cause. On a more personal level, on several occasions lack of parental supervision has provided unrestricted access to loaded weapons which adolescents have used to perform mass shootings of innocent victims.

Influenced by Political, Religious or Social Agendas

Political, religious and social agendas can have a powerful effect on the propensity for disastrous outcomes. Risks can arise when those in a position to exercise religious, political or social authority purposely place individuals and groups at risk by implementing oppressive policies and tactics to control behavior.

When these agendas are overly strict and constraining, with little room for dialogue and compromise, affected parties may react by resorting to extreme and sometimes hostile measures, thereby creating an additional set of risks. Consider student demonstrations that attracted over one million protesters to Beijing's Tiananmen Square in the Spring of 1989, calling for democracy, free speech and free press in China. Rather than serving as a catalyst for social reform, Chinese authorities declared martial law and ordered the military to conduct a bloody crackdown on the demonstrators, killing hundreds of innocent victims and injuring thousands of others.

An important observation when reviewing these underlying risk factors is that we, as humans, have an active role in every one of them. While this means that we contribute to the cause or impact of virtually every disaster, it also means that we have an opportunity to control these factors more effectively to achieve a better outcome.

An important observation when reviewing these underlying risk factors is that we, as humans, have an active role in every one of them.

So, where do we begin? A good place to start is to carefully review undesirable events which have occurred in the recent past, selecting a potpourri of those that were accidental, intentional or due to natural causes. If we can follow the sequence of actions that caused the unfortunate outcome and analyze what went wrong, then we can extract important "lessons learned" about how to better control these risk factors in the future. We can then apply these lessons proactively to stave off making the same mistakes again. We'll talk more about these lessons in a later chapter.

An Enterprise Risk Management Perspective

A common phrase bandied about these days is the term *new normal.* The argument is that when circumstances have taken on a transformation, it is no longer a special condition, but rather what we should come to expect. It follows then that we must shift our view of these situations as no longer aberrations, but rather business as usual and plan accordingly.

What is interesting about managing risks in a new normal environment is that the process is fundamentally similar to how it *should* have been practiced in the past. It has just moved more into the limelight as the need for risk-informed decision-making has become accentuated. This is driven by the unprecedented number of risk-related events with catastrophic outcomes we are experiencing, with the prospect of this trend continuing and likely growing. It has sensitized us to the notion that natural and human-induced perils can originate in many ways and that we need to be vigilant in controlling them to the best of our abilities.

What is interesting about managing risks in a new normal environment is that the process is fundamentally similar to how it *should* have been practiced in the past.

More so than ever before, this begs for a systematic approach, one that considers all factors and scenarios that threaten our ability to function as desired in relation to our risk appetite. This all-hazards approach has been given the moniker of *enterprise risk management* (ERM).

There are a variety of reasons for why practicing ERM makes good sense. ERM enhances the safety and security of ourselves and others, improves the quality of our decisions and reduces surprises by being more risk-informed, controls unnecessary expenditures by treating risks before they become more costly problems, creates opportunities for competitive advantage, helps grow a proactive culture that recognizes and rewards problem avoidance, and increases outsider confidence in our attitudes and behaviors.

Earlier, I mentioned the term *risk appetite*. Our risk appetite refers to how much risk we are willing to accept when faced with a potentially threatening situation. If we judge the risk to fall within our risk appetite, it means that we are willing to accept that risk as is, without feeling the need to exercise additional control. Conversely, if the risk exceeds our appetite, it signals that we should take action to reduce the risk to a level that is acceptable relative to our appetite.

Everyone has a risk appetite and it can vary depending on the threat and opportunity. We may be more risk averse when facing certain situations and more risk prone regarding others. It is important to acknowledge the concept of a risk appetite and apply it when making risk-informed decisions.

Everyone has a risk appetite and it can vary depending on the threat and opportunity.

Within an ERM approach, our risk appetite can be defined by key risk indicators (KRIs) that help guide decision-making. KRIs measure the status of each of the items in our risk portfolio. They can take on many forms, such as accident rates, credit card debt, and school grades, to name a few.

When a KRI exceeds the threshold as established by our risk appetite, it indicates a need to take some type of risk management action. Ideally, we would like to consider implementing risk reduction strategies that we can accomplish within our own resources, such that we can control how the strategy is introduced and managed. Procuring cybersecurity software or installing motion detectors on a building are examples of these actions. If these options are not possible or insufficient, another approach is to transfer the risk somewhere else; obtaining an insurance policy is a form of risk transfer. Finally, if neither of these approaches are able to satisfy our risk appetite, we can decide to avoid the activity that is posing the risk altogether. Cancelling a cruise due to concerns over exposure to COVID-19 would fall into this category.

There is a structured process to adopting an ERM perspective. It is centered around answering the following foundational questions, which I refer to as the *risk quartet*:

- What can go wrong?
- How likely is it?
- What are the consequences?
- What, if anything, needs to be done to reduce our risk (satisfy our risk appetite) within available resources?

Let's discuss these steps in the order they appear, beginning with *what can go wrong*. This is the most important step in the ERM process, because if we are unable to identify all potential scenarios of what can go wrong, the missing ones are ignored completely, leaving us vulnerable even if we apply the proper ERM principles to those scenarios that are identified. To guard against this possibility, it is important to cast the net wide in terms of scenario creation.

From a business perspective, the risks can be broad and include both scenarios that the organization can control as well as those beyond its control. There is no prescription for what to include on the list, nor a one-size-fits-all approach. However, generally the following business risks may be present, listed in no particular order:

- Competition – The competition gains advantages that prevent us from reaching our goals.
- Economic status – Conditions in the economy increase our costs or reduce sales.
- Employee health & safety – Our workplace has known health and safety hazards.
- Infrastructure & equipment – Our infrastructure or equipment fails to perform as desired.
- Customer relations – Customers are dissatisfied with our product and/or service.
- Operational – Our daily work processes are not well established or incorrectly applied.
- Community – Our organization is not viewed as a good corporate citizen.
- Environment – Our activities threaten ecological well-being.
- Supply chain – We are unable to source materials necessary to maintain business continuity.
- Legal – Our organization faces liabilities and legal disputes.
- Regulatory – There is potential for us to be exposed to new regulations or violate existing regulations.
- Reputational – We are suffering from a declining reputation or loss of public confidence.
- Innovation –We may become obsolete due to the introduction of new technologies or business practices.
- Credit – Entities who owe us money fail to re-pay.
- Exchange rate – Volatility in foreign exchange rates impacts the value of our transactions and assets.
- Interest – Changes to interest rates cause a business disruption.
- Taxation – Tax laws or interpretations cause us to experience a higher-than-expected taxation.

- Resource –Business goals are not met due to lack of resources such as financing or skilled labor.
- Social and political – Social and political events impede our business activities.
- Natural hazard – Extreme weather, earthquakes and other natural hazards cause us to suffer excessive loss and damage.
- Public health – Pandemics and other health crises impede our business operations.
- Security – We suffer breaches in cyber and/or physical security, including potential loss of intellectual property or trade secrets.
- Opportunity – Effort is expended that results in wasted time, energy or resources.

While every item on this list, and perhaps others, requires thorough understanding and regular review, certain ones are likely to be more prominent at a particular point in time. For example, public health risk associated with COVID-19 helped cause a severely disrupted global supply chain, coupled with a worker shortage that forced some businesses to close or reduce operations. Businesses who fail to anticipate such risks ahead of time or lack the agility to adapt in real-time are particularly vulnerable.

Enterprise risk management from a personal perspective should encompass situations that are potentially encountered as part of daily life. Individuals and families face many of the same perils as organizations, although these risks may differ in how they manifest themselves and their associated impacts, as noted below:

- Competition – Your competition gains advantages that prevent you from reaching your personal goals.
- Financial – Negative outcomes are associated with your investments, taxes, interest rates, refinancing, recession, liquidity and other financial management practices.

- Safety – An accident or crime impacts your health or quality of life.
- Property – You experience problems with housing, equipment and other property that you depend upon.
- Reputational – Fractured relationships occur with family, friends, business associates or the community at large.
- Business – Risks threaten the viability of a business owned by you or your family.
- Operational – Daily routines constrain your ability to achieve desired goals.
- Environment – You fail to implement sustainable practices and protect the environment.
- Career – You incur job loss, salary reduction, or other negative outcomes in your career due to action or inaction.
- Legal – You have personal liabilities or are engaged in legal disputes.
- Resource – You are unable to meet your personal goals due to lack of resources.
- Social and political – Social and political events and outcomes impede your livelihood.
- Natural hazard – Loss and damage are incurred due to extreme weather, earthquakes and other natural hazards.
- Health – Life choices and illnesses threaten your physical and mental health.
- Security – Harmful breaches impact your cyber or physical security.
- Opportunity – Effort you expend results in wasted time, energy and resources.

The aforementioned list of business and personal risks, and any others that may be relevant, form the basis for constructing scenarios where these risks may become reality. The scenarios themselves rely on understanding the different risk factors that may play a role in how these perils could manifest themselves.

As described in the previous chapter, common factors that singularly or in tandem may serve as root causes for risks to emerge include:

- Design or construction flaws
- Deferred maintenance
- Schedule or financial constraints
- Ignoring the plight of socially vulnerable populations
- Communication failure
- Lack of planning or preparedness
- Inadequate legal/regulatory standards or compliance
- Lack of training or experience
- Complacency
- Arrogance or greed
- Lack of oversight
- Influenced by political, religious or social agendas

To create a specific risk scenario worthy of consideration, one might select a relevant business or personal risk, and then identify the risk factor(s) whose occurrence would enable that risk to become a reality.

Here are a few examples of how this process would work:

- You are renting an apartment in a building where a greedy landlord purposely defers maintenance on a faulty smoke alarm system in order to maximize his profits. A fire ensues, endangering your life and causing personal property loss, including the destruction of prized possessions.
- Social unrest in a developing country grinds commerce to a halt, leaving your business unable to source necessary supplies.
- Failure to communicate a developing severe storm leaves elderly and impoverished residents unable to seek safe shelter, resulting in unnecessary human casualties.

Scenario creation is an open-ended exercise that should not be shortchanged, even if it leads to a relatively long laundry list of what could go wrong. Later in the ERM process you can eliminate or diminish the importance of some risk scenarios based on their likelihood of occurrence, impact and your risk appetite.

Failure to maintain a broad perspective while performing scenario creation can lead to a catastrophic outcomes. Consider the September 11, 2001 terrorist attack on the World Trade Center and the Pentagon. While security officials were focused on scenarios where terrorists would use sophisticated means to hijack an airplane, nobody apparently foresaw the possibility of a low-level technology – box cutters – as the weapon terrorists might use to commandeer an aircraft.

Failure to maintain a broad perspective while performing scenario creation can lead to catastrophic outcomes.

Once risk scenario creation is complete, the ERM process moves to the next step, determining the likelihood that a particular scenario may occur. If detailed information is available, one can be precise in determining likelihood; for example, there is a 63% chance that the event will happen. However, for practical purposes and when information is more limited, scenario likelihood can also be characterized as belonging to subjective (or qualitative) categories, such as:

- Virtually Certain
- Very Likely
- Even Odds
- Unlikely
- Remote

Critical to answering the likelihood question is the time frame over which the risk is being assessed. For example, a risk scenario may be remote if considered over the coming month, but virtually certain over the coming decade. Time frame is especially important when considering large investment projects that are expected to have an extended useful life. Such is the case for the construction of a new bridge, where the design is based on the bridge having a useful life of 50 years or more. In this instance, it may be judged that a major natural hazard event, perhaps a high-intensity hurricane, is virtually certain to occur during the expected life of the bridge.

In its basic form, risk is considered the outcome of likelihood and consequence (impact). The previous ERM process step examined the likelihood of occurrence of each risk scenario. The companion step is to consider the impact if the event actually takes place.

Scenario consequences are typically measured in terms of loss and damage (L&D). Loss is commonly defined as the negative impacts in which restoration or reparation is impossible, whereas damage refers to impacts for which restoration or reparation is possible. L&D are generally separated into categories of tangible and intangible. Tangible L&D can be further sub-divided into direct and indirect impacts. Tangible direct L&D are considered consequences incurred as a direct result of the physical impact of the event, such as damage to infrastructure or property loss (e.g., buildings, cars, livestock, crops). Fatalities and injuries are often included in this category. Tangible indirect L&D would be consequences that occur as a result of a direct impact. Examples include business interruption, relief efforts, lost tourism, relocation costs, disruption to transportation, and diminished living conditions.

Intangible impacts are effects felt by society, but for which the accompanying L&D is difficult to value monetarily. Mental distress, long-term health effects (e.g., cancer), cultural identity, environmental quality (e.g., habitat degradation, wetland destruction), and territory abandonment would be included in this category. It could even extend to impacts associated with customer satisfaction, employee confidence, creditworthiness and reputation.

As in the case of evaluating scenario likelihood, one can attempt to develop a precise estimate for L&D, yet for practical purposes, one may prefer to assign L&D for a scenario to a general category, such as:

- Minor
- Moderate
- Major
- Severe
- Worst Case

Note that each of us may have a different perspective on what constitutes a particular category of scenario likelihood or impact. For example, you may consider virtually certain to be an event that will definitely occur, while I may believe that any event likelihood of 90% or more defines that category. Similarly, what you consider as moderate L&D may be viewed as severe by somebody else. For example, $100,000 in direct tangible L&D might be considered minor by a wealthy person or organization, whereas it may be viewed as severe for someone with limited assets.

Once each risk scenario has been assessed according to its likelihood and impact, we can position every scenario on a common platform to identify the subset of those risks that exceed our appetite and therefore require immediate or more prolonged attention. This is conveniently done by creating a *risk heat map*, essentially a plot showing where each scenario sits relative to its likelihood and impact, similar to what is shown below.

A risk scenario of grave concern would be located in the upper right-hand corner of the map, because it has been judged to be virtually certain to occur and when it does, will render considerable harm. Conversely, a risk scenario located in the lower left-hand corner would be viewed as an event that has little chance of occurrence and if it did, would result in a minor impact.

IMPACT \ LIKELIHOOD	Remote	Unlikely	Even Odds	Very Likely	Virtually Certain
Worst Case	Yellow	Red	Red	Red	Red
Severe	Yellow	Yellow	Yellow	Red	Red
Major	Green	Yellow	Yellow	Yellow	Red
Moderate	Green	Green	Yellow	Yellow	Red
Minor	Green	Green	Green	Yellow	Yellow

Sample Risk Heat Map

Note that in this risk heat map image, each cell has been assigned a green, yellow or red color. This is a useful way to sort out how to respond to each scenario relative to our risk appetite. If a risk scenario falls into a green cell, the risk is considered under control without the need to consider an intervention. A risk scenario that lands in the yellow zone would be viewed as having the potential to develop into a more significant concern; while immediate intervention may not be necessary, the scenario requires careful monitoring should it increase in likelihood or consequence. Finally, a risk scenario landing in a red cell implies that it poses a significant enough threat that immediate risk mitigation action is warranted.

One has considerable latitude in what color to assign to each cell. In the above example, note that cells colored in red include scenarios where the event is virtually certain and the consequences are moderate, as well as where the event is unlikely but the consequences would be catastrophic. In the former case, the rationale for assigning a red color is that if the scenario is essentially guaranteed to occur, even if the consequences are beyond minor, shouldn't we do something about it? In the latter case, although the event is deemed highly unlikely, it nevertheless remains plausible and should it occur, the results would be disastrous, potentially life-threatening or ruining a business; is that a chance we are willing to take? The decision of how to color the boxes is ultimately a personal choice.

The final component of the risk quartet addresses the question of what can be done, if necessary, to lower our risk within available resources. The desired goal is to identify risk mitigation strategies that land in the sweet spot of being affordable, provide a significant risk reduction benefit, and likely achieve its intended purpose.

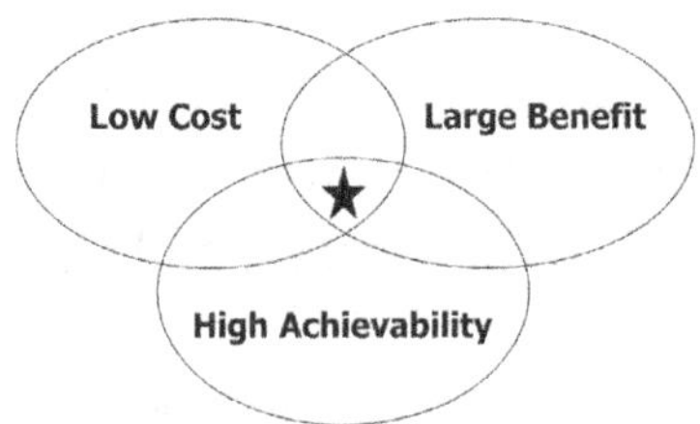

Finding the Risk Mitigation Strategy Sweet Spot

This last consideration, achievability, is often overlooked by risk analysts. In the past, there have been countless proposed risk reduction strategies that appear to be relatively low in cost and offer a large benefit, yet when examining the idea more closely, it stands little chance of being successfully implemented. Take for example a proposed risk reduction strategy to increase the size of a community's police force, the justification being that the extra police presence will reduce crime to a historical low, well worth the investment. However, it would require the approval of the town board, which is strapped for cash and not in a position to re-allocate funds from another budget item. A great idea in principle, but not achievable.

It is equally important to take a closer look at risk reduction strategy costs and benefits. In assessing the cost of strategy implementation, we must not only realize the upfront costs to launch the strategy, but also the ongoing expenses associated with maintaining the strategy over its intended lifetime. This is particularly true for risk reduction strategies that involve substantial investment in infrastructure, as maintenance and repair costs could be big ticket items, particularly as the infrastructure ages.

When examining strategy benefits, one should be mindful of who will benefit, with a particular nod towards whether socially disadvantaged populations are being treated equitably. We must also be keenly aware of when the benefits will accrue, such as whether they are limited to immediate effects or are sustainable and able to deliver value for extended periods of time.

An additional caveat about benefits is the extent to which they may prove their worth beyond their targeted impact. Imagine a situation where a community considers a risk reduction strategy to invest in a tornado alert system, thereby giving residents extra time to seek safe shelter, with the benefits justified in terms of saving lives. However, suppose this same alert system could be used to notify residents of situations involving child abductions, active shooters, chemical releases, flash floods or wildfires. Arguably, the added benefits of reducing these risks should be included in the assessment of the overall benefits of investing in what was originally conceived as solely a tornado risk mitigation strategy.

Finally, as mentioned several times in earlier chapters, evaluation of benefits and costs would be remiss without considering unintended consequences. While it may seem that the majority of the time unintended consequences put a drag on strategy benefits, it is also possible for those consequences to provide added value. For example, from sourcing a stronger material for the manufacture of a certain product, a company might discover that this material can be used to development an entire new line of merchandise.

For those candidate risk reduction strategies deemed to warrant active consideration, the final step is selection of the most desirable strategy or strategies to implement. Similar to the risk heat map introduced earlier, one can construct a *risk reduction strategy heat map*. It differs from the previous introduced risk heat map, however, in that the parameters are risk reduction benefit and risk reduction cost, as shown below.

STRATEGY BENEFIT \ STRATEGY COST	Very High	High	Moderate	Low
Very High	*Very Good*	*Very Good*	*Excellent*	*Excellent*
High	*Good*	*Good*	*Very Good*	*Excellent*
Moderate	*Fair*	*Good*	*Good*	*Very Good*
Low	*Fair*	*Fair*	*Good*	*Very Good*

Sample Risk Reduction Strategy Heat Map

Note that the values for risk reduction cost are reversed; that is, a high cost is less desirable while a low cost is preferred. If a candidate risk reduction strategy lands in the upper right-hand corner of this map, the prospect for it to be successful is excellent, as it has been assessed as having high benefit and low cost. Conversely, a high-cost risk reduction strategy with relatively small benefit would land in the lower left-hand corner of the map and likely dropped from consideration. As shown in the figure, it can be handy to separate the map into cells to help bring the assessment process into sharper focus, with the user having considerable latitude in what designation to assign to each cell.

◆ ◆ ◆

By considering the risks we encounter in an enterprise (all hazards) manner, each potential threat can be identified, evaluated and prioritized. Out of this process can come prudent decisions of where and how to invest available resources to reduce those risks of greatest concern. Moreover, by managing our risks under a single enterprise-wide umbrella, there may be opportunities to reduce a specific risk while simultaneously diminishing other risks.

ERM can be performed by governments, businesses, communities and individuals alike, based on respective concerns and the risk management decisions that one can control. Moreover, there are several advantages if the process can be implemented in a way that is inclusive with other parties who influence or are affected by these risks. Better ideas and solutions can be generated, there is a greater transparency and understanding of what is being done to reduce risk, and there is increased confidence that the outcome will be successful.

ERM can be performed by governments, businesses, communities and individuals alike ...

The overarching takeaway from this discussion is that we need to stretch our minds more broadly in thinking about what can go wrong, and be better prepared to manage those scenarios in a proactive rather than reactive way. You may remember the Fram Oil Filter advertisement from many years ago in which the mechanic says, "You can pay me now or you can pay me later", where *now* is a relatively small preventative cost in comparison to *later*, after a major breakdown has occurred. Let's take that message to heart.

Lessons Learned

It is not necessary for history to repeat itself. A silver lining arising from prior misfortunes is that what we learn could reduce the likelihood or severity of a similar occurrence in the future. Not only does this help us understand what went wrong and how to mitigate problems experienced in the past, it can also provide a basis for imagining future disaster scenarios that might arise.

Be wary of the danger, however, in being conditioned to focus exclusively on situations that have occurred in the past. Historical recordkeeping is relatively short when compared with the frequency of potentially catastrophic events that may occur rarely and therefore are not on our radar. Some events may even be unprecedented. Also, social, economic and environmental conditions are changing at such a rapid pace that we cannot exclusively rely on the past as a predictor of future impacts, even from the same event.

Adopting this approach to risk management can be guided by the lessons learned from what we have previously experienced. Most important is the following:

Life is an inherent choice among alternative risks.
Life is risk. Risk is imminent and can never be completely eliminated. Nothing can be designed to perfection nor last forever, and we need to accept that. Every minute of every day, somewhere in the world, people are hurt, property is damaged and the environment is harmed. Sometimes the impact is felt by a few people at a specific location, while in other cases the impact can involve mass casualties or cover a large expanse. No matter how hard we try to create a safe and secure environment, it is not humanly possible to make it entirely risk-free. Even if we had unlimited resources to invest in our safety and security, there is no assurance that nothing bad will happen.

> Life is risk. Risk is imminent and can never be completely eliminated.

Therefore, we must recognize that life is an inherent choice among alternative risks. The key to successfully managing these risks is being able to identify and assess them, enabling us to prioritize what to try to control. We can then direct our attention and resources at reducing, albeit not eliminating, those risks of greatest concern. For these reasons, we must adjust our outlook and expectations about the level of protection we can realistically expect. Simply put, we need to become more tolerant of certain risks and recognize that sometimes bad things will happen even when we put our best foot forward, and that is just a fact of life.

Within the context of this paramount observation, the following lessons form a foundation to establish risk management best practices. They are presented in no particular order of importance.

Lesson 1: Risk factors typically work together to generate an event with disastrous consequences.
Problems usually arise due to a variety of risk factors; rarely is one factor solely accountable. Most of life's activities come with a built-in margin of safety. We create this buffer to feel a level of comfort that we will be alright even if something might go wrong. This usually works pretty well should a single risk factor go awry, as the built-in safety margin is likely to absorb this glitch and still protect us from an adverse outcome. Levels of protection like this include technologies that warn us of a developing problem which can be corrected before it leads to failure, a redundant capability to perform the same function as back-up, or the existence of a contingency plan to limit the damage if the problem cannot be contained.

When a disaster occurs, however, it is likely that multiple developments have gone wrong, completely eroding our margin of safety and leaving the situation to spiral out of control. Therefore, limiting the number of risk factors in play will improve the chances that our margin of safety will remain intact.

Consider the case of a large metropolitan area located on the coast, which is subject to frequent hurricanes and corresponding damaging winds and storm surge. To prevent extensive flooding, the city has erected a large levee to keep water from reaching the community. Should the levee fail, the city has massive pumps that are capable of removing flood waters before the area is inundated. A storm hit the city one day with such intensity that it overwhelmed the levee and water poured into the city. Unfortunately, high winds that accompanied the storm knocked out power such that the pumps were rendered inoperable. Disaster ensued. Had the levee held or the pumps worked properly, it would have resulted in little to no harm. By having both risk factors emerge simultaneously, the built-in margin of safety disappeared and the results were catastrophic.

Lesson 2: You can rarely communicate too much.

The inability to share important information that is timely and accurate is a common theme in virtually every unfortunate outcome. This risk factor can either be attributed to the cause of an undesirable event, the severity of the outcome, or both.

Communication failure is a complex problem, however, as it can involve man or machine. Failure can be attributed solely to an equipment problem, such as system overload (e.g., jammed phone lines), poor reception, interoperability of different communication devices, or lack of technology. Failure can also occur if certain individuals neglect to pass along vital information, do not think it is important to do so, or delay in making it known. The proliferation of misinformation, accidental or intentional, is commonplace as well. Transfer of misinformation can occur between individuals, within an organization, between organizations, or between authorities and the general public.

Having to act on misinformation or no information can make risk decision-making a fragile proposition. Communication failure was a major factor that led to the space shuttle Challenger disaster in January 1986. Engineers at Morton-Thiokol, a contractor working for NASA, were aware that an O-ring, designed to prevent hot exhaust gas from escaping from inside the booster, would not perform properly at low temperatures. This information was shared with Morton-Thiokol senior management, but apparently did not reach NASA officials. As a result, a decision was made to launch Challenger under unusually cold weather conditions. Shortly after takeoff, the O-ring failed, causing a chain reaction that eventually led to an explosion aboard the spacecraft and loss of the entire crew. In hindsight, armed with this information, NASA may have delayed the launch until more favorable weather conditions, and this disaster may have been avoided altogether.

Lesson 3: Take planning and preparedness seriously.
Along with communication failure, one of the most commonly experienced risk factors is the lack of planning and preparedness. Effective planning and preparedness are based on careful consideration of various scenarios describing what might go wrong, likelihood of occurrence, and potential consequences should the event transpire. Risk mitigation strategies can then be devised to address these scenarios before problems arise.

Yet all too often we jump into taking action without proper planning and preparedness, placing unnecessary stress on trying to make difficult decisions in a timely manner when a crisis has arisen without the necessary information to back it up. Equally culpable are situations where one has made a concerted effort to be properly prepared, yet this information has gone stale or is gathering dust on a shelf without anyone remembering the pre-existing effort.

We discussed earlier the consequences associated with a haphazard approach to planning and preparedness for the emerging COVID-19 pandemic. This is just one of the latest of a long line of disasters that might have been averted if planning and preparedness had been taken more seriously, creating opportunities for a proactive rather than reactive response. In reviewing a variety of recent disasters, natural and manmade alike, think about what we have learned in hindsight about indications that something bad might happen that were simply ignored. Imagine what might have been done if this information was brought to light prior to when the situation devolved.

Lesson 4: Relenting to economic and schedule pressures can prove devastating.

When someone is strapped for resources or faces an upcoming deadline, the added stress can change their decision-making behavior in ways that magnify risk. Often, they yield to these pressures by avoiding spending on risk mitigation actions or cutting corners on existing safety and security protocols to keep from falling further behind.

While there are a variety of past events where economic and schedule pressures have produced a catastrophic outcome, each of us can think of poor decisions we have made in response to economic and schedule pressures, in some cases being fortunate that it didn't lead to an ensuing problem, while in other cases perhaps not so lucky. Every time we bust a red light, cross a railroad track without pausing to ensure there is no oncoming train, or travel on highways far in excess of the speed limit, it is likely a maneuver to get somewhere as soon as possible in response to a schedule pressure. And every time we forego making a major car repair, removing or trimming a tree that overhangs the house, or deferring replacement of an aging furnace, it can be attributed to an economic consideration that might ultimately lead to a risky outcome.

Lesson 5: Religious, political and social considerations impact how one manifests and reacts to risk.

It is virtually impossible to imagine a high-risk situation that is not seeded in some way by a religious, political or social issue. We have repeatedly witnessed intentional acts of destruction that originated in response to a religious, political or social condition where a suppressed individual or group concluded there was no other recourse than to initiate a hostile action. Moreover, if the event cause may not have been religiously, politically or socially motivated, response to the crisis was heavily influenced by these considerations.

This bias also exists in countless situations where preferential treatment is given to helping certain groups in times of crisis. Those who suffer are more likely to be socially vulnerable populations, discriminated against according to their age, race, gender, ethnicity, income or political affiliation. Social discrimination is readily apparent in the lack of access of the poor to quality health care. Religious fervor has been the catalyst for the start of many conflicts that have been further exacerbated in war-torn nations where this zeal has led to heinous crimes against humanity. Political discrimination manifests itself in laws and policies that favor a specific population while targeting another.

Lesson 6: Don't underestimate the role of arrogance and greed as risk factors.

Individuals in a position of authority and organizations with a mandate to perform a certain function are particularly susceptible to developing arrogant and greedy behavior. When this power is left unchecked, it provides a fertile environment for encouraging abhorrent behavior. It is important to recognize the potential for circumstances to arise that are conducive to arrogance and greed, both in acknowledging the risk introduced by this behavior and in devising strategies to mitigate the risk to the extent possible. Having adequate oversight and establishing checks and balances are important risk mitigation strategies to implement.

Instances of greed can be more malicious in that while arrogance may be reflective of disregard for doing the right thing, greed is knowingly acting to do the wrong thing. It doesn't take much to think how greed has affected our personal or professional well-being. Anytime someone or some organization exercises their authority to take more for themselves and give less to everyone else is indicative of why greed is such a powerful risk factor. Lack of access or availability of resources can have profound effects on our social, economic or environmental fabric.

Lesson 7: Many risks we don't think about on a daily basis deserve our regular attention.

In navigating through daily life, we may not be routinely exposed to every threat that comprises our risk portfolio. We may believe certain risks to be under control or there is little need to monitor the situation. Taking such a cavalier outlook, however, can obscure the possibility that these risks are gaining prominence over time. It is important to monitor our entire risk portfolio on a regular basis and stay educated on current events that may alter our perception of what we thought to be a benign situation. By taking this steadfast approach, a developing problem is more likely to be recognized in its infancy, at a time when it can be acted upon with less effort and reduced anxiety.

Consider the following scenario. Suppose you recently renewed your home insurance policy, believing that this ensures protection of your most important financial asset from the threat of flood, fire and high winds. Each year, upon renewal, you carefully stash away the latest policy in a folder to show that your premium has been paid. The fine print in the relatively large policy document is too much trouble to review, so you naturally assume that your coverage has not changed. When a massive flood subsequently inundates your basement and first floor, you are surprised to discover that a recent policy change has placed a cap on the remuneration you can receive, which doesn't come close to the amount of damage incurred. Much to your chagrin, when the policy change was made, you had ignored instructions to purchase a special rider to expand the coverage limit if so desired.

In many respects, this lesson is intertwined with complacency. Whereas we want to stay abreast of prospective risks on a daily basis, if we have experienced a problem in the past that was successfully addressed, we tend to believe the problem has been eradicated. Over time, we can become complacent to the point of ignoring the fundamentals that caused the prior problem to be resolved, creating a greater possibility of reoccurrence.

...if we have experienced a problem in the past that was successfully addressed, we tend to believe the problem has been eradicated.

Lesson 8: As some risks are more important than others, we must learn to prioritize.

For an individual or an organization, not every risk is created equal. Each of us can articulate a slew of risks we might encounter, but they differ in terms of those that are more important to our well-being and under what circumstances. Rising to the top should be risks that are frequently encountered or whose consequences are serious, albeit if the likelihood of that outcome may be somewhat rare. Assuming there is a limit on the physical, financial or mental resources to tackle them all, we must prioritize those risks of greatest concern for which there exist practical and achievable solutions, and we have adequate resources available.

Suppose you know someone who operates a Ma and Pa restaurant in a suburban location which has been exceptionally hard hit by the COVID-19 pandemic. In normal times, the restaurant is popular among the lunch business crowd and for family dining in the evening. The owners typically make a modest profit, which they have stashed away to spend once they retire. With declining revenues from fewer patrons due to COVID-19, they face a choice of: 1) laying off workers who have been extremely loyal, or 2) depleting their retirement nest egg to keep their core team employed and hope for better days ahead. The first option may keep the restaurant alive, but by furloughing workers, these employees will be exposed to a risk of financial hardship. If the owners select the second option, they will forego any personal financial security in return for mitigating the risk of financial hardship for their employees and keeping open the possibility of returning to profitable operation. The owners elect to choose Option 2, prioritizing the desire to manage their employees' financial risks rather than their own.

Lesson 9: All risk factors contain a human element, meaning that every event is either preventable or the impacts can be contained.

Over the course of history, covering calamities occurring in different places around the globe, both manmade and natural, and affecting different infrastructure sectors and populations, one thing stands out. In every instance, human intervention could have mitigated some or all of the risk had it been properly handled. In some cases, better decision-making could have prevented the incident from occurring at all, while in other instances the event consequences could have been marginalized. Although we humans have been culpable for such failures, it also presents opportunities to intercede with well-developed risk decisions that have a positive impact.

Lesson 10: Successful risk management is a continually evolving process that is embedded in a strong safety culture. Successful risk management practices do not happen by chance. Rather, they are the culmination of considerable investment in planning, preparation and ongoing engagement. None of this is possible without an underlying culture within an organization or family unit that is committed to safety first.

Creating and maintaining a strong safety culture can be challenging, however. It is rather easy to claim that we have made this commitment, but quite another matter to walk the talk. Safety first implies that it is the bottom line, even if at times it means greater cost and lost opportunity. And safety first cannot be treated as a special project or temporary campaign. To be successful, everyone at the lowest level of responsibility to the very top should be empowered to adopt this philosophy as a fundamental component of daily practice.

Consider an individual who began her career as a front-line worker on a car assembly line. After a few weeks on the job, she noticed a problem with how the parts were provided to her for assembly, making it likely that she might receive the wrong part for the vehicle model, which in turn could lead to an operational safety problem. She mentioned this concern to a co-worker, who agreed that the problem existed, but cautioned against saying anything, recalling that the last time an assembly line worker voiced a concern, they were unceremoniously fired.

This prompted the individual to quit her job and find employment in a similar role for another car manufacturer, one with a reputation for having a strong safety culture. She immediately noticed that certain safeguards were in place that prevented her from receiving the wrong parts. When sharing this observation with a co-worker that such safeguards did not exist at her former job, the co-worker explained that at one time they had a similar concern and reported it to management. Not only was the process changed to mitigate the problem, but the person who originally reported the problem received an award for helping the company improve its safety performance.

Lesson 11: There may be unintended consequences to risk mitigation strategies that can make matters worse.
Jumping the gun to implement a risk mitigation strategy can end up backfiring if attention is not devoted upfront to studying the potential for unintended consequences. Not thinking through the entire scenario prior to implementation can result in placing people and organizations at greater risk than if nothing is done at all.

Fortunately, unintended consequences were considered several years ago prior to instituting a U.S. government policy that would have required all children, regardless of age, to occupy their own seat on commercial air travel (rather than sitting on an adult's lap). If this policy had gone into effect, families traveling with small children would have been forced to purchase a separate seat for their child. The unintended consequence of this policy is that families unable to afford an extra seat would instead choose to travel by car. An ensuing study concluded that more lives of children would be lost from accidents associated with additional car travel than would be saved by having small children sitting by themselves on the aircraft. As a result, this policy was not enacted.

Lesson 12: The best way to manage risk is through an integrated approach of prevention, response and recovery.
Any risk management strategy that diminishes incident likelihood or reduces the consequences should the event occur is considered an asset to one's well-being. Therefore, the gold standard risk management program is one that should be directed at all phases of the risk spectrum, recognizing that opportunities to achieve risk reduction could avail themselves at any point in the disaster timeline.

Consider the following situation. The chief risk officer (CRO) for an oil pipeline company realized that a major oil spill would have grave economic and environmental impacts, jeopardizing the future viability of the business and causing irreparable harm to the pristine environment in which the pipeline is located. In contemplating how to minimize this possibility, the CRO realized a risk management frontal assault would be needed, focused collectively on prevention, response and recovery.

The CRO tackled this challenge by first developing plausible scenarios for how a leak could occur and devising corresponding prevention strategies. She knew, however, this would not guarantee that a leak could be fully prevented, so she reviewed the company's capabilities to provide an immediate and effective response under such circumstances, and saw opportunities for improvement. Further, the CRO reasoned that even if the response was timely and effective, under certain conditions the business could still suffer a sufficiently large disruption that a strategy was also needed to recover to normal operations as soon as possible.

In presenting his overall plan to the company board, the CRO stated, "We have reduced the likelihood that the company will experience a leak, but should the unlikely happen, we have enhanced our ability to respond in a timely and effective fashion. Further, should we suffer a business disruption despite our best efforts, my proposed recovery strategy will bring us back on-line in short order. The bottom line is that we have greatly improved our ability for the business to thrive while being a good corporate citizen to the environment." Board members concurred with the CRO's assessment and her proactive approach to problem-solving.

Lesson 13: It is important to set reasonable risk thresholds and to review them on a regular basis.

Everyone has a risk appetite, one in which we consciously or subconsciously establish a level of risk we are willing to incur for the reward we are seeking. If the risk we confront for the reward being sought is within our appetite, then we consider seeking that reward as worthwhile. However, if we perceive the risk to be greater than the reward, our risk appetite has been exceeded and we decide the reward is not worth pursuing, or at least not without some intervention.

Everyone has a risk appetite.

One's risk appetite can differ for people seeking the same reward. Consider the opportunity to be an astronaut on a space mission. A reward like this could prompt some of us to pursue this opportunity regardless of the risks involved (i.e., unlimited appetite), while others may shy away from pursuing the opportunity altogether, or perhaps unless certain proven safeguards are in place.

As we are constantly witnessing changes to our environment, it is good practice to review our risk appetite and thresholds on a regular basis. What constitutes a regular basis will differ for each of us, but is likely to be based on a unit of time, say annually, or as the result of an important event, such as a personal or professional achievement or loss.

Lesson 14: The lack of timely and decisive leadership during a crisis is a risk magnifier.

Leaders need to lead, especially when their constituents are facing a crisis situation. Great leaders confront crises by making timely and decisive risk-informed decisions. Ineffective leaders may give the appearance they are acting in a responsible fashion, but below the surface there is little to show for their rhetoric. The difference between strong and ineffective leadership can translate into large numbers of casualties, economic turmoil, social unrest, and loss of public trust. When placed in a position of leadership, the ability to uphold safety when faced with dire circumstances should be foremost in mind.

When the COVID-19 outbreak began, many believe then President Trump was derelict in providing leadership during a time of national and global crisis. Critics cite his unwillingness to treat COVID-19 immediately as a serious public health threat, abdication of the federal role as leader of the nation in combatting this crisis, and taking few, if any, decisive actions when problems with the pandemic became widely known. They argue that this lack of timely and decisive leadership caused the pandemic to spread more rapidly and over an extensive period of time, helping to proliferate millions of infections, hundreds of thousands of casualties, high unemployment, and considerable family suffering.

Lesson 15: Managing risk will nearly always involve compromises based on weighing benefit and cost.
How safe is safe enough? This is a fundamental question pondered by individuals, organizations and society at large. There are two approaches to answering this question. One approach is to argue that we can never be safe enough until we reach a point of zero risk, a fallacy because it is impossible to ensure that something unfortunate will never happen. The alternate outlook is to view "safe enough" as a continuous pursuit to lower risk as long the benefits exceed the costs with each marginal risk mitigation investment. This latter approach makes more sense as it is couched in reality; however, it places a burden on finding solutions that meet the criteria of being cost-effective, practical and achievable.

A situation that has garnered considerable attention involves the extent to which investment in coastal flood protection is justified in terms of using taxpayer money to foot the bill. Suppose the cost of installing a flood wall is judged to do little to ensure the safety of the community from storm surge expected with future hurricanes. Such an investment would therefore not meet the "safe enough" standard, as the cost exceeds the benefit, and some other strategy, perhaps permanent relocation, should be entertained instead.

Lesson 16: Do not ignore the plight of socially vulnerable populations.

There are many more socially vulnerable populations than we might imagine when it comes to understanding risks that these groups face and the limited resources they have available to manage those risks. These groups may be defined by their socioeconomic status, household composition, disability, minority affiliation, immigration status, language proficiency, housing type or transportation mobility. And it is not difficult to imagine the many people with multiple socially vulnerable characteristics among this list.

More often than not, socially vulnerable populations reside in higher risk locations, be it areas with increased criminal activity, where floods are more likely to occur, or devoid of basic essential services (health care, law enforcement, communication, food, energy, water, transportation). Consequently, they are placed at a tremendous disadvantage in terms of the likelihood of experiencing unfortunate events and the ability to withstand the resulting impacts.

As a society, we have a moral imperative to care for the physical and mental health of the socially vulnerable. Adequately addressing their risks requires a philosophy that they deserve as much consideration as anyone else to be resilient in the face of threats imposed on them. This translates into developing risk management strategies that recognize the special needs of various socially vulnerable groups, and provide an equitable amount of planning and resources to create a safety net they deserve. This is in stark contrast to focusing disproportionately on the risk management needs of the well-to-do, with those of socially vulnerable populations as a mere afterthought.

What is remarkable about these lessons is that they are easy to understand and make practical sense. Moreover, they can be put into regular use by individuals and organizations alike.

What is remarkable about these lessons is that they are easy to understand and make practical sense.

The foundation of successful risk management is planning, preparedness and communication. This forms the basis for establishing sound daily practices that involve a commitment to a strong safety culture, while managing activities that do not impose unreasonable economic and schedule pressures. Pay attention to how things are designed, built and maintained. Recognize certain individuals and organizations may be politically, religiously or socially motivated, as well as arrogant or greedy in ways that could undermine your well-being. And understand that risk factors often work together to create a crisis, so beware of circumstances where these factors can become intertwined or have cascading effects.

What we want to avoid is having to experience a disastrous event before concluding that adopting an approach like this is warranted. We don't want to be so engrossed in our daily lives that an important problem is ignored until a catastrophic event wakes us up and makes us take notice. By only then recognizing the need for reform and taking appropriate action, we have already paid a high price that could have been averted.

Heeding these lessons will carry you a long way towards a safer future. However, adopting this approach does not guarantee it will work every time. Remember, risk is inherent in life.

Your Risk Dashboard

A helpful way to keep orderly track of the risks you care to manage is to prepare and maintain a summary statement of your current risk portfolio, organized according to where threats currently stand and where they may be heading in the future. I call this your *Risk Dashboard.*

Your risk dashboard does not have to be a complicated formula or graphic that takes lots of time to assemble, update and interpret. Rather, its simplified nature is what makes using a risk dashboard a worthwhile endeavor.

Below is an example of a risk dashboard template that illustrates how this can be done. It consists of just four columns: 1) risk category, 2) current risk status, 3) direction the risk is trending, and 4) what risk mitigation actions, if any, you have implemented or should be taken.

Risk Category	**Status**	**Trend**	**Activities**
[List risks under consideration]	• Green • Yellow • Red	↓ ↘ ↔ ↗ ↑	[List risk mitigation strategies in place or recommended for implementation]

Green: Acceptable Risk

Yellow: Monitor Risk

Red: Risk Mitigation Needed

↓ Significant Risk Reduction

↘ Marginal Risk Reduction

↔ No Change

↗ Marginal Increase in Risk

↑ Significant Increase in Risk

Risk Dashboard Template

Your relevant risk categories can be defined to be as general or specific as you desire. For example, it could be as general as "natural hazards" or as specific as "tornados". Most importantly, ensure that what you list is consistent with your perceived risk, risk appetite and ability to manage.

Risk status represents your assessment of the level of concern you associate with a specific risk at the present time. A convenient way to assess risk status is to use a qualitative measure that is easy to understand. The use of colors, particularly *red*, *yellow* and *green*, correlate well with the way we approach these signals when driving in traffic. Green would indicate the risk is either not that imposing or sufficiently under control that no immediate action is needed. Yellow is equivalent to "proceed with caution", meaning that the situation warrants monitoring in case it changes, although no immediate action may be necessary. Finally, red sounds an alarm that the risk is currently at such a heightened level that immediate action is required.

The direction a risk is trending is equally important. This indicates whether, since the last dashboard update, the risk has leveled off, is moving in a direction requiring greater attention, or is showing signs of being brought under control. Of utmost concern is a risk with a red status that is trending upwards, meaning that an already serious problem is posing an even greater risk than previously encountered. In these circumstances, prompt action is required to mitigate the problem before the situation spins any further out of control. Conversely, a red risk status that is trending downwards indicates that although the situation may be improving, the risk has still not reached an acceptable level and further mitigation action should be considered.

Similar logic can be applied to risks whose status are assessed as green or yellow, and are trending in one direction or another. For example, a risk currently characterized as yellow, but trending in an upward direction, should be recognized as an emerging threat that warrants careful monitoring. Conversely, a yellow risk that is trending downward suggests that potential for an undesirable event is waning, albeit still worthy of keeping an eye on.

Note also that a risk may actually change color categories from one assessment to the next. Sufficient progress or deterioration may have occurred such that the risk has moved beyond the direction it had been trending to occupy a different place in your risk priorities, either higher or lower.

The activities column is used to track risk reduction measures already in operation or to recommend implementation of additional strategies. Where a risk mitigation strategy is already in place, the dashboard serves as a basis for determining whether the strategy is working, something that is reflected in the current status of the risk and how it is trending. If the risk status has moved from red-to-yellow or yellow-to-green, or is trending downward while maintaining the same risk status, one can surmise that the measure is having a positive effect. On the other hand, if there has been a deteriorating change in risk status or is trending towards increased risk, additional measures may be warranted. When this is the case, the actions column should include a list of additional strategies for implementation consideration.

The beauty of a risk dashboard is that it works equally well for individuals and organizations. While the types of risks will differ and each individual and organization will have a unique risk appetite, it provides the ability to assess the status of each risk, how it is trending, and what actions, if any, are in place or in need of implementation. An added benefit is that the risk dashboard can be bundled, such that dashboards developed by respective divisions of a company can be combined to represent, in the aggregate, a corporate perspective. A similar situation could apply to an individual, where the roll-up of individual risk dashboards can form a family perspective.

> **The beauty of a risk dashboard is that it works equally well for individuals and organizations.**

Organization Risk Dashboard

The table below presents the risk dashboard for a hypothetical organization. In this example, risks of concern have been grouped into general categories, reflective of the overall exposure of the business to these considerations.

This organization has identified six risk categories in its portfolio: 1) avoiding business disruption, 2) maintaining a satisfactory level of cybersecurity, 3) protecting the health of its employees, 4) having a robust balance sheet, 5) remaining competitive in the marketplace, and 6) being resilient when threatened by natural disasters.

The organization's risk dashboard places *business interruption* risk in the red zone, but is showing that prior mitigation strategies are helping to reduce this risk. One action is to keep those strategies in operation and allow more time to see if their full effects have been realized. Rather than waiting, since the overall risk is currently in the red zone, the organization believes that immediate implementation of additional risk reduction strategies is warranted. The recommended measure is to negotiate additional contracts with suppliers of critical raw materials so that if the primary supplier cannot deliver on time, the organization has a backup plan to maintain business continuity.

Risk Category	Status	Trend	Activities
Business Interruption	Red	↘	• Continue implementing prior risk mitigation strategies • Implement new strategy to establish redundant supply chain options
Cybersecurity	Red	↑	• Continue implementing prior risk mitigation strategies • Hire consultant to review current cybersecurity program • Explore new technologies to improve security firewalls
Employee Health	Yellow	↗	• Review employee health benefits plan and personal leave policy
Financial Volatility	Yellow	↔	• Monitor key financial performance indicators
Market Competition	Green	↘	
Natural Disasters	Green	↗	

Sample Organization Risk Dashboard

Cybersecurity is also listed in the red zone and, unlike business interruption, this risk has increased significantly. It is due to the fact that the organization experienced a recent breach that caused a large amount of data to be compromised, even though several security strategies had been implemented that were thought to be effective. To rectify the situation, the organization plans to implement two additional strategies: 1) hire a consultant to provide a critical review of the organization's current cybersecurity program, and 2) explore new technologies that may afford the company improved firewall protection.

The situation with *employee health* risk is not considered as serious, listed in the yellow zone. However, due to a rise in infectious disease transmission and concern that employees are disgruntled regarding sick leave policies, risk for this category is increasing. A rising yellow risk has motivated the organization to take a cautionary position for fear of losing situational control unless it takes proactive action, in this case reviewing its employee health benefits plan and personal leave policy.

Financial volatility, although also currently labeled as a yellow risk, can be treated somewhat differently since it is trending flat, meaning that the risk is neither growing nor diminishing from the previous review. As a result, the organization is maintaining a monitoring activity as opposed to the more proactive posture being taken with respect to employee health risk.

Market competition risk is not only considered to be in the green zone, but the risk is also declining. No further action is therefore needed at this time. *Natural disaster* risk has also been placed in the green zone, although this risk is on the rise, due to growing concern over the potential for more frequent and severe extreme weather events. However, this concern has not reached a point where natural disaster risk is judged to fall in the yellow zone. Hence, while no action is being taken at this time, there is enhanced awareness that this situation will need to be re-visited as part of the next review cycle.

Another helpful way to use dashboard results is to plot risk categories together on a graph, similar to the one shown below. Presenting the status and trend of all risk categories on a common platform can help an organization visualize the results. On this graph, the x-axis represents risk status and the y-axis represents risk trend. Any risk category located towards the lower left-hand portion of the graph is one that is under control and improving. By contrast, a risk category that appears in the upper right-hand part of the graph is distressing and becoming even more problematic, indicating a dire need for risk management intervention. While containing the same information as in the risk dashboard template, presenting results in this visual form can assist in evaluating the overall status of a risk portfolio and help determine how to utilize available risk management resources.

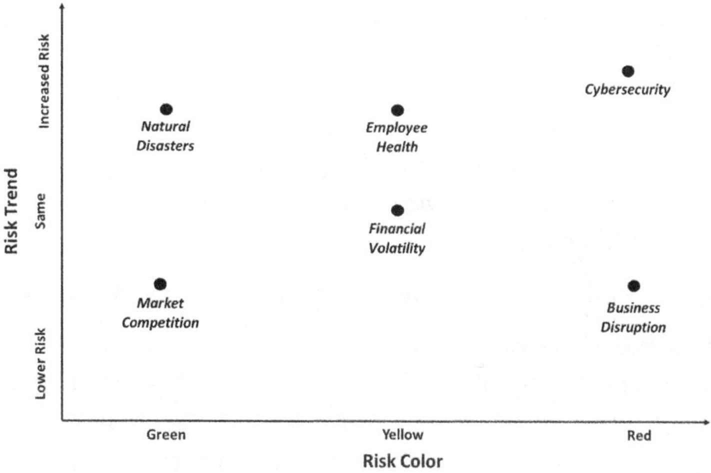

Sample Company Risk Dashboard Graphic

Individual Risk Dashboard

A sample individual risk dashboard appears below. Note that the format is identical to the dashboard table for an organization. While the risk categories in this example reflect what is on the individual's mind, the approach is just as systematic and logically sound as that of an enterprise.

Risk Category	Status	Trend	Activities
Career Development	Green	↔	
Crime	Yellow	↘	• Neighborhood Watch program now fully implemented
Extreme Weather	Yellow	↗	• Obtain information on past extreme weather events in my area and future climate forecasts
Finances	Yellow	↓	• Mortgage refinancing completed
Information Security	Red	↘	• Continue utilizing multiple cybersecurity apps • Check for new updates
Mental Health	Red	↑	• Continue mental health counseling and medications • Join a support group

Sample Individual Risk Dashboard

This individual has also selected six categories to manage: 1) career development, 2) crime, 3) extreme weather, 4) finances, 5) information security and 6) mental health. Note that there is no magic number of categories one may generate; it is up to the individual or organization to determine based on their unique situation.

Career development risk is important to this individual. Fortunately, they feel comfortable with the current employment situation and growth opportunities such that no action is required at this time.

Personal safety is also highly valued, so any threat of *crime* would be worrisome. This individual has assigned a risk status in the yellow zone, but also feels that their community is becoming safer, due to the fact that a recently established Neighborhood Watch program is now in full operation and results to date have been positive.

The situation is somewhat different regarding *extreme weather* risk. Although this risk remains in the yellow zone, it is increasing. Similar to employee health risk in the organization risk dashboard example, the increasing risk trend is prompting the individual to decide to become more knowledgeable of the type of extreme weather events they are likely to experience in the future.

Finance risk is a cornerstone of maintaining a comfortable lifestyle for this individual. However, while still viewed as a yellow zone risk, it is trending in an improving direction, owing to having recently refinanced their home mortgage with a lower interest rate.

Risk associated with *information security* remains a red zone threat, albeit the situation is improving. Having been hacked several times in the past, the individual has, as a risk reduction strategy, invested in several cybersecurity apps. While they appear to be working, the individual plans to remain vigilant by keeping current with any software updates to safeguard against newly discovered software breaches.

The final risk category, *mental health*, poses the greatest concern. This risk has remained in the red zone from the previous dashboard review and it is exhibiting a disturbing trend. This individual, having experienced the loss of a loved one and a personal health crisis, is dealing with anxiety and depression. Although they are receiving mental health counseling and taking prescription medications, their coping skills are in decline. Joining a support group has been identified as an immediate action to help rectify the situation.

Similar to the organization example, a visual representation of the individual's risk dashboard can prove useful. As shown below, emphasis on the need for mental health risk mitigation stands out.

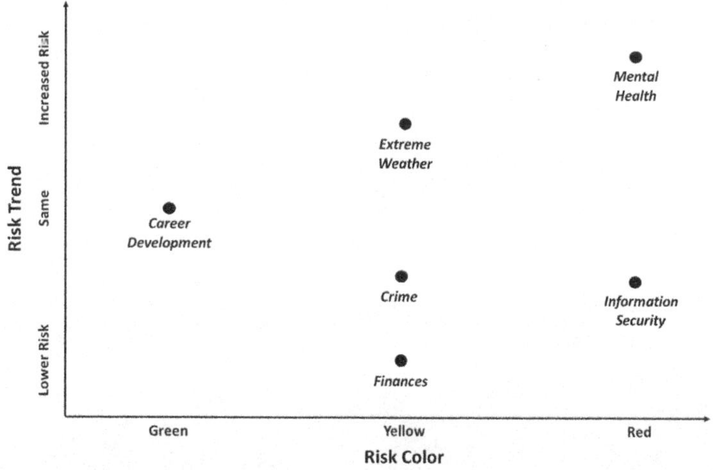

Sample Individual Risk Dashboard Graphic

Maintaining a risk dashboard is a handy way to monitor and address the risks impacting an organization or individual. The dashboard is simple to organize and update, yet serves as a powerful risk management tool. Its beauty lies in the ability to categorize and customize risks, using qualitative metrics (color, trend) to monitor status and movement. Moreover, dashboard results can be presented in a tabular or graphic form that are easy to understand and can serve as a useful means for communicating risk to others. How often one updates the dashboard is a matter of personal preference. This could take place on a routine basis (e.g., monthly, quarterly, annually) or when a significant event has occurred that immediately alters a prior assessment (e.g., extreme weather event, financial loss, public health crisis).

A risk dashboard is simple to organize and update, yet serves as a powerful risk management tool.

Rules of Engagement

In the last few chapters, we have explored the ingredients for establishing a principled foundation for managing risk, one that is designed with practicality and ease-of-use. Moreover, this approach can be customized to reflect personal circumstances and evolving situations.

In reviewing painful past experiences, we have learned that protecting our future cannot be left to chance. Not every risk factor will be present in every situation we confront, nor will they be valued the same. Yet, we have also observed that although unfortunate events come in many forms, their respective risk factors and outcomes have much in common. This provides strong justification for adopting an enterprise approach to risk management, one that is holistic and systematic.

It's always helpful to boil down a complex subject into a set of simple guidelines to follow, and managing risk is no exception. Below are ten rules of engagement to live by as you formulate your risk portfolio and take action to "stay on the wall".

1. **Don't let media hype cause you to overreact.**

Breaking news.....there is no breaking news! Wouldn't that be a wonderful headline? Unfortunately, this won't happen anytime soon, because the media feeds on sensationalizing any story it can to get us hooked. And we have proven to be susceptible to this strategy. We are far too easy prey nowadays with the advent of 24/7 coverage of events taking place around the world, complete with video. With a global population of over 7 billion people, something catastrophic is virtually guaranteed to happen every day somewhere on the planet. By acknowledging this reality, we can put media hype in the proper context, and be selective in relying on those sources we consider credible and relevant to our risk portfolio.

2. **Judge whether your perception mimics reality.**

Are your fears justified? Have you verified that credible information supports your level of concern? The optics around risk perception are extremely powerful and we tend to be motivated by fear. For this reason, many risks are overrated while others deserving greater attention fly under the radar. Knowledge is power in these circumstances, and it is incumbent on each of us to confirm that our risk perception aligns with reality. Recognize, however, that exercising sound judgement can be hindered by human emotion, such that practicing a disciplined approach is necessary to succeed at this endeavor.

3. **Assess how likely it is to impact you.**

There is no limit to the risks that may be present at any given time. What truly matters is the extent to which a particular risk is impactful to your well-being. Does it matter if you can get seriously hurt when surfing if you are not a surfer? Should you care if rampant floods are occurring, yet you do not live near a floodplain? The takeaway message here is to think about the commensurate amount of energy you should spend focusing on a particular threat.

4. **Consider what is at stake.**

Don't sweat the small stuff. More than likely you have heard this expression before. But have you actually taken it to heart? We live in a fast-paced world where much is happening around us, coming from all directions and at seemingly warp speed. In order to avoid more than you can handle, take a step back and ask whether the issue at hand is such a big deal. You may be surprised at how much of what you might worry about is actually noise rather than something of substance. By considering what is at stake, you will be better positioned to avoid getting caught up in the frenzy and instead free to concentrate on risks that are truly worthy of your attention.

5. **Determine what you can control.**

When deciding whether to engage in certain activities, often that decision is made by implicitly agreeing to cede control to someone else. Such situations abound, for example as a passenger in a car, airplane, train, boat or other form of transportation, sitting in a building constructed by someone else, or using products manufactured elsewhere. Ask yourself how sensible it is to worry about those things that you can't control. If it causes that much angst, then perhaps it would be best to avoid the situation altogether. Otherwise, accept the circumstances as part of your risk appetite and instead worry about things you can control.

6. **Recognize the potential for unintended consequences.**

Far too often, decisions are made to mitigate a risk without thinking through the full ramifications. Many transportation departments regret a decision made decades ago to plant kudzu to help prevent erosion on slopes around highways. Little thought was given to whether introduction of this invasive species might totally overwhelm all native vegetation in the area. One should carefully consider what might go wrong when attempting to solve the initial problem, as the unintended consequences could present a greater risk than what was originally being experienced.

7. **Evaluate how you may be trading off short-term gain for long-term pain.**

Instant gratification rules the roost these days. We feel compelled to address a problem right away to satisfy our need for immediate satisfaction; otherwise, we have failed. Yet it is precisely this short-sightedness that can contribute to more serious outcomes at a later time. Often, the quick fix only addresses the symptom of a problem rather than its root cause. Be careful not to fall into this trap. Rather, think about the time frame over which the problem may be present and act accordingly with the big picture in mind. There can be a lot of wisdom in the adage, "Haste makes waste."

8. Keep an eye on the horizon.

While there is considerable value in learning from history of what has gone wrong in anticipation of what to expect in the future, that perspective alone is not sufficient. History tells us much about status quo and whether certain types of risks are trending up or down, but it cannot anticipate how the world will react to changing conditions that are unprecedented. For this reason, we must consider future scenarios that are reasonably foreseeable, based on what might happen if certain circumstances prevail. Climate change could be the poster child in this category, where predictions of future temperature and precipitation could seriously alter the landscape in terms of sea level rise, storm surge, flooding, drought, wildfires and other calamities we have yet to witness. The other "elephants in the room" we discussed earlier pose similar challenges. The point here is that a savvy risk manager applies knowledge of the past with a realistic view of what the future may bring in order to keep a keen eye on the ball.

9. Live life in moderation.

For the time we have on this planet, there is little sense to walk around constantly worrying that the sky is falling, nor does it make sense to put our life on the line by being the world's greatest daredevil. There is plenty of room in between to find a comfort zone, where our risk appetite is compatible with life's pleasures. The key is to take stock of what makes us happy and to manage the risks that accompany that lifestyle. By living life in moderation, we can achieve a balanced portfolio of risks and rewards.

10. Accept that no matter what you do, bad things can happen.

Our lives are fulfilled when we make risk-informed choices that allow us to reap the rewards without incurring negative effects. Yet, because bad things can happen that are beyond our control, there is no guarantee that even if we make all of the right choices, we will always avoid the mishaps. When these situations arise, of course it makes sense to reflect on what went wrong and to question whether adjustments to our risk behavior should be made. But sometimes we may merely have to shrug our shoulders, accept the consequences, and keep plugging away.

While by no means the be all and end all, by applying these rules of engagement, it's a good bet that you will be more satisfied with what you can achieve while keeping the risks you encounter in check. It is all about the choices we make and how we go about making them.

Final Thoughts

At the outset of our journey, we established that our world is a complex and volatile place, and that each of us is a Humpty Dumpty, living a fragile existence fraught with all kinds of threats and vulnerabilities. We also observed that although we may be perched on different walls facing varying levels of peril, we all face situations that could upend us, with the possibility of falling off our wall and having great difficulty, if ever, recovering from the impact. To not only survive, but to potentially thrive, we explored the need to adopt a perspective and an approach that keeps us balanced while simultaneously being able to enjoy the view. Protecting our future does not have to be left to chance.

Although risk has always been and will always be an inherent part of life, our circumstances require navigating through a risk landscape that is far more complicated than what our predecessors encountered, bombarded from many directions and at a frenetic pace. It begins with establishing a greater awareness of what shapes our risk perceptions, a willingness to make adjustments where it makes sense to re-calibrate in seeking a healthier perspective, and understanding how our risk appetite leads to corresponding behaviors.

We also acknowledged the importance in considering how individuals and organizations we interact with form their risk perceptions. When communicating risk with others, it is essential to customize our narrative such that it demonstrates an appreciation and respect for their needs, and a willingness to communicate in an honest, candid and open manner. Otherwise, odds are the conversation will devolve into becoming so contentious that finding common ground becomes impossible and long delays are incurred before the matter can even be brought forward again for possible resolution.

We must also be mindful of being misled by the information we receive, sometimes even when obtained from supposedly credible sources. And cognizant that while rates are important for measuring the respective risk of an individual who is associated with a specific statistical group, rates alone should not be the basis for deciding what merits your risk management attention. Frequencies are also important, as while rates may indicate the risk to a specific individual, if the population of the statistical group is sufficiently large, there may be greater impacts involving that group overall even if the rate is relatively low. Moreover, we must be mindful that our demographics, activities and activity levels all play a role in increasing or decreasing our exposure and vulnerability, and consequently the risks we incur, with socially vulnerable populations particularly susceptible to these effects.

While being aware of what has occurred in the past and what we encounter today, it would be a grave error not to project into the future. Ignoring a world that is undergoing such rapid transformation, with new threats constantly emerging, could have troublesome ramifications. These "elephants in the room" are serious business, including those we have singled out in this book:

Extreme weather and climate change - Making an immediate and compelling effort to strengthen our management of extreme weather and climate risk is a necessity and no longer an option if we want our society to survive.

Cybersecurity - While our reliance on the internet has provided numerous benefits, it comes at the cost of unintended consequences in the form of cybersecurity vulnerability, be it crime, espionage or warfare.

Social networking - With social networking an obsession and our addiction to its trappings, we must be wary of an outside world that can be harmful, whether by accident or malicious intent.

Infectious diseases - The emergence of future infectious diseases with the potential to reach pandemic levels are likely to become more frequent, placing the onus to be vigilant and proactive in our approach to mitigate this risk.

Domestic terrorism - This is a serious and growing threat, and difficult for intelligence agencies to identify and track perpetrators until they render harm, knowing that ever-evolving social, political and religious crises will spawn additional terrorist acts.

Geopolitical conflict – With geopolitics a fixture in today's world and beyond, our livelihood depends on our ability to identify emerging conflicts and to reconcile them before they manifest themselves into civil disobedience and hostility.

These elephants in the room also serve to exacerbate and further erode an already fragile society exhibiting signs of *declining mental health*. The connection between risk and stress can spawn many forms of mental health disorders. To confront the devolving process by which these risks influence our perceptions, emotions and behaviors, we can establish a healthier means of managing risk by recognizing and acting on the stress triggers before they erupt, practicing "risk hygiene" so to speak.

What we concluded from reviewing underlying factors that create risky situations is that humans have an active role in all of them. This creates opportunities to assert greater control over these factors towards achieving a better outcome. Success comes in part by learning from prior misfortunes, lessons that can help us understand how to confront today's challenges, while also preparing for future threat scenarios.

The foundation of successful risk management is planning, preparedness and communication. It forms the basis for establishing sound daily practices that involve a commitment to a strong safety culture, while managing activities that do not impose unreasonable economic and schedule pressures. Pay particular attention to detail of how things are designed, built and maintained. Recognize that certain individuals and organizations may be politically, religiously or socially motivated, acting with arrogance or greed in ways that could be detrimental to others. Understand that risk factors often work together to create a crisis situation, so be on the lookout for circumstances where these factors can become intertwined or have cascading effects. While not every risk factor will be present in each situation we confront, nor will they be valued the same, as long as we are aware of their presence and understand their importance, effective measures can be taken.

And there are tools at our disposal to make this transformation a reality. By applying an enterprise approach to risk management, we are better positioned to make intelligent choices about which risks to try to control, avoid or accept. We have also been introduced to the notion of a risk dashboard as a simple and handy tool for describing, monitoring and addressing the risks that reside in our portfolio at any given time.

Lastly, remember that while adopting Humpty's approach will make for a less vulnerable and more resilient lifestyle, there is no guarantee that success will always be achieved. We will suffer at times. It can happen when we do everything in our power to control a situation, yet it isn't good enough. Or a lower priority risk we elected not to address yields an unlikely destructive event.

The bottom line is that we can and should do better at being a master rather than a victim of risk. All it takes is a more organized approach to managing the risks that affect our daily lives, coupled with a greater tolerance for unfortunate events that will sometimes happen no matter how hard we try. It is a matter of understanding those risks, weighing the pros and cons, and making good choices.

There is an old adage that, "nothing is certain, except death and taxes". It is time that we add a third item to the list – risk. After all, life is risk. But if we do the right things, we no longer need to be driven by fear. The reward, peace of mind, is well worth the effort.

Chapter References

Communicating Risk

"Ashland Oil fined $2.25 million for spill that fouled two rivers", *L.A. Times Archives.*

"The 1988 Monongahela oil spill", *Archives of the Pittsburgh Post-Gazette.*

What Should I Worry About?

"Odds of dying", *National Safety Council.*

"Mortality in the United States", *National Center for Health Statistics.*

"Number and rate of fatal work injuries, by private industry sector", *U.S. Bureau of Labor Statistics.*

Adapting to Climate Change and Extreme Weather

"Weather and atmosphere", *National Oceanic and Atmospheric Administration.*

"Sixth assessment report", *Intergovernmental Panel on Climate Change.*

"Heat forecast tools", *U.S. National Weather Service.*

"Extreme heat", *U.S. Centers for Disease Control and Prevention.*

"Collaborating to improve community resiliency to natural disasters", *Tennessee Advisory Commission on Intergovernmental Relations.*

"Wildfire and climate change", *United States Geological Survey.*

"WCRP coupled model intercomparison project", *World Climate Research Programme.*

"Collective action in communities exposed to recurring hazards: the Camp Fire, Butte County, California, November 8, 2018", *Natural Hazards Center.*

Grappling with Cyber Security

"Complaints and losses over the last 5 years", *U.S. Internet Crime Complaint Center.*

"The facts", *U.S. Cybersecurity and Infrastructure Security Agency.*
"Dating site hackers expose details of millions of users", *The Guardian.*
"Adult Friend Finder and Penthouse hacked in massive personal data breach", *The Guardian.*
"Hackers breached Colonial Pipeline using compromised password", *Bloomberg.*
"U.S. recovers $2.3 million in ransom paid to Colonial Pipeline hackers", *CBS News.*
"Meat processor JBS paid $11 million in ransom to hackers", *New York Times.*
"Facts and statistics: identity theft and cybercrime", *Insurance Information Institute.*
"Cyberwarfare, cyberactivism, internet worm, password manager", *Technopedia.*
"What is cyber espionage", *Crowdstrike.*
"Cyberactivism, its past and its future", *Digital America.*
"Five times Internet activism made a difference", *Christian Science Monitor.*
"Stop ransomware", *Cybersecurity and Infrastructure Security Agency.*
"Back to basics: multi-factor authentication", *National Institute of Standards and Technology.*
"Cyber security training for employees", *Travelers.*
"Password security best practices", *Business2Community.*
"Internet crime report", *Federal Bureau of Investigation.*
"SolarWinds was the subject of a massive cybersecurity attack that spread to the company's clients", *Business Insider.*
"Report identity theft and get a recovery plan", *Federal Trade Commission.*

Avoiding the Dark Side of Social Networking

"How to manage risks of AI", *Gates Notes.*
"The pros and cons of social media", *Lifewire.*
"Is social media good for society?", *Britannica.*
"Most popular social networks worldwide", *Statista.*

"Ice bucket challenge dramatically accelerated the fight against ALS", *Amyotrophic Lateral Sclerosis Association.*
"Corporate activism is more than a marketing gimmick", *The Conversation.*
"Artificial intelligence pros and cons: what are the advantages and disadvantages of AI", *rockbottom.*
"The impact of AI on social media", *TechTarget.*

Combatting Infectious Diseases
"The worst epidemics and pandemics in history", *Live Science.*
"Health topics", *World Health Organization.*
"Africa's approaches to crisis management are unique when it comes to dealing with disease", *World Economic Forum.*
"Global impact of human immunodeficiency virus and AIDS", *National Library of Medicine.*
"Rapid response was crucial to containing the 1918 flu pandemic", *National Institutes of Health.*
"Cholera", *World Health Organization.*
"Severe acute respiratory syndrome (SARS)", *Centers for Disease Control and Prevention.*
"What you need to know about infectious disease", *National Library of Medicine.*
"Black Death", *History.*
"1918 pandemic (H1N1 virus)", *Centers for Disease Control and Prevention.*
"The 1918 flu is still with us: the deadliest pandemic ever is still causing problems today", *The Washington Post.*
"What is HIV?", *Centers for Disease Control and Prevention.*
"The worst outbreaks in U.S. history", *Healthline.*
"Polio", *The College of Physicians of Philadelphia.*
"Ebola virus infection", *WebMD.*
"Coronavirus disease (COVID-19)", *World Health Organization.*
"Herd immunity and COVID-19: what you need to know", *Mayo Clinic.*
"Food & water precautions", *Centers for Disease Control and Prevention.*

"COVID 19: people with certain medical conditions", *Centers for Disease Control and Prevention.*
"Outbreaks, epidemics and pandemics—what you need to know", *Association for Professionals in Infection Control and Epidemiology.*
"Endemics, epidemics and pandemics", *Physiopedia.*
"COVID-19: long-term effects", *Mayo Clinic.*

Fighting Domestic Terrorism
"The military, police, and the rise of terrorism in the United States", *Center for Strategic & International Studies.*
"The war comes home: the evolution of domestic terrorism in the United States", *Center for Strategic & International Studies.*
"Terrorism", *Federal Bureau of Investigation.*
"Strategic intelligence assessment and data on domestic terrorism", *Federal Bureau of Investigation.*
"Annual threat assessment of the U.S. intelligent community", *Office of the Director of National Intelligence.*
"September 11 attacks; Waco siege; Tulsa race massacre", *History.*
"Sandy Hook school shooting; Terrorist gunman attacks Pulse nightclub in Orlando, Florida", *History.*
"How many people in the U.S. own guns?", *American University Radio.*
"Wall Street bombing 1920", *Federal Bureau of Investigation.*
"Black Wall Street was shattered 100 years ago - how the Tulsa race massacre was covered up and unearthed", *CNBC.*
"3 hours in Orlando: piecing together an attack and its aftermath", *National Public Radio.*

Risk and Mental Health
"How extreme weather events affect mental health", *American Psychiatric Association.*
"Climate change's toll on mental health", *American Psychological Association.*
"Mental health and the COVID-19 pandemic", *The New England*

Journal of Medicine.
"The implications of COVID-19 for mental health and substance use", *Kaiser Family Foundation.*
"Anxiety, loneliness and fear of missing out: the impact of social media on young people's mental health", *Centre for Mental Health.*
"Preparing for the psychological consequences of terrorism: a public health strategy", *National Library of Medicine.*
"The impact of the Paris terrorist attacks on the mental health of resident physicians", *BMC Psychiatry.*
"Anxiety, depression and PTSD: The hidden epidemic of data breaches and cybercrimes", *USA Today.*
"Mental health and cybersecurity," *U.S. Cybersecurity Magazine.*

Risk Factors
"Fatal and nonfatal falls, slips, and trips in the construction industry", *U.S. Bureau of Labor Statistics.*

An Enterprise Risk Management Perspective
"Enterprise risk management", *Corporate Finance Institute.*
"Enterprise risk management framework", *Johnson & Johnson.*
"20 types of business risk & 17 examples of personal risk", *Simplicable.*

ABOUT THE AUTHOR

Mark Abkowitz

Mark Abkowitz is a Distinguished Professor at Vanderbilt University who specializes in risk assessment, management and communication, with a focus on threats, vulnerability and resilience. He has led numerous studies involving mainstreaming risk management into individual and organizational behavior through easy-to-use, actionable methods and practices. Dr. Abkowitz has served on numerous national and international advisory committees, including as a Presidential appointee, and is currently Chair of the National Academy Sciences Committee on Extreme Weather and Climate Change Adaptation. He has written numerous articles and spoken at a variety of conferences, in addition to appearing on national television, radio, and podcasts. Dr. Abkowitz is also the author of a critically acclaimed book entitled Operational Risk Management – A Case Study Approach to Effective Planning and Response.

BOOKS BY THIS AUTHOR

Operational Risk Management: A Case Study Approach To Effective Planning And Response

Operational Risk Management offers peace of mind to business and government leaders who want their organizations to be ready for any contingency, no matter how extreme. This invaluable book is designed to be used as both a preparatory resource for when times are good and an emergency reference when times are bad. Author Mark Abkowitz gets managers up to speed on what they should be prepared to deal with and offers real solutions for putting those buisness continuity plans in place. From natural and man-made disasters to terrorist attacks, Operational Risk Management is destined to become every risk manager's ultimate weapon to help their organization survive - no matter what.

Made in the USA
Monee, IL
15 August 2025

22397161R00118